HANDLE WITH
PRAYER

HANDLE WITH
PRAYER

Unwrap the Source
of God's Strength
for Living

CHARLES
STANLEY

transforming lives together

HANDLE WITH PRAYER
Published by David C Cook
4050 Lee Vance View
Colorado Springs, CO 80918 U.S.A.

David C Cook U.K., Kingsway Communications
Eastbourne, East Sussex BN23 6NT, England

The graphic circle C logo is a registered trademark of David C Cook.

Unless otherwise noted, all Scripture quotations are taken from the King James Version of the Bible. (Public Domain.) Scripture quotations marked NASB are taken from the *New American Standard Bible*, © Copyright 1960, 1995 by The Lockman Foundation. Used by permission.

LCCN 2010940571
Hardcover ISBN 978-0-7814-0446-4
Paperback Edition ISBN 978-1-4347-0944-8
eISBN 978-1-4347-0317-0

The Team: Alex Field, Amy Kiechlin, Sarah Schultz, Jack Campbell, Karen Athen
Cover Photo: iStockphoto

Printed in the United States of America
Paperback Edition 2011

4 5 6 7 8 9 10 11 12 13

052416

CONTENTS

1

UNVEILING THE HIDDEN

Moreover the word of the LORD came unto Jeremiah the second
time, while he was yet shut up in the court of the prison,
saying, Thus saith the LORD the maker thereof, the LORD that
formed it, to establish it; the LORD is his name; Call unto
me, and I will answer thee, and show thee great and mighty
things, which thou knowest not. —Jeremiah 33:1–3

As I was praying one afternoon in 1967, I began feeling as if God
had something very specific to say to me. The more I prayed, the
more the burden increased. I decided to take an early vacation and
spend the time seeking God's guidance. I went to the mountains
of North Carolina for two weeks, intent on finding out what God
was saying to me.

I spent the majority of the time fasting and praying. I waited,
expecting God to follow up the burden with an answer. To my

surprise, He pointed out areas in my life that needed correcting. The entire two weeks was a period of personal cleansing and preparation for what was to come.

I returned home excited, but still unsure. It was as if there were a veil that kept me from knowing the unknown. I felt that the answer was close, but it was still out of my grasp. Then one afternoon soon afterward, I was on my face before the Lord, and the veil lifted. God wanted me to start a school. I hesitated to commit myself to such a task, but God made it clear to me that His instructions were to be *obeyed*, not just considered. He unveiled the hidden to me when I called on Him to do so, and He showed me the things I did not know. God was faithful—even to the point of preparing my heart for what He had to say.

God desires to make known the unknown to His children. He desires to unveil the hidden. Yet many times we are satisfied not knowing. Either we aren't willing to take the time to wait, or we aren't sure God even wants us to know. But this command to Jeremiah speaks specifically to both of these problems. We are to call, we are to expect an answer, and we are to know the unknown. Let's look at the background of this Scripture in Jeremiah (33:1–3).

The Babylonians are coming toward Jerusalem from the east. They have already defeated the Assyrians, so the people of Jerusalem know they don't stand much of a chance against their superior military strength. The leaders of Jerusalem believed they should align themselves with the Egyptians, which was the logical thing to do. But Jeremiah tells them, "God says you are going into captivity. What you really ought to do is go out there and surrender." Well, this wasn't at all what the leaders had in mind. They threw Jeremiah in prison and refused to listen to him.

Their reaction should not surprise us. What do you think the people in my congregation would do if I stood up next Sunday and said, "God says the Canadians are going to overthrow this nation. We might as well surrender now and save ourselves some trouble"? They would run me out of town! But this was exactly the situation Jeremiah found himself in. From his experience, he gives us a passage (33:1–3) that helps us understand how to talk with God.

Encouraged to Pray

We can obtain three prayer principles from Jeremiah 33:3 by listening to what God told Jeremiah. The first is that God encourages us to pray: "Call unto me." Since Jeremiah was in prison, he had a long time to catch up on his prayer life. We may never be put behind bars, but God will put us in circumstances and situations in order to teach us how to talk with Him.

Most of the time we pray, "Get me out of here!" We want to avoid suffering and difficulty. When we *do* run into a trial or difficulty, we ask God to change our circumstances so we can serve Him better and love Him more.

But we cannot fool God or bribe Him with our promises. Jeremiah didn't even ask God to get him out of prison. Rather, he waited to see what God would say to him. And what was God's reply? "Call unto me, and I will answer thee, and show thee great and mighty things, which thou knowest not" (Jer. 33:3). What

God did for Jeremiah had a far greater impact than simply getting him out of prison.

But most of us aren't that patient. We're more intent on getting out of our circumstances than we are on finding out what great things God wants to show us. But the Father never allows difficulty just for the sake of difficulty—there is always a higher purpose involved. The problem is we cannot always identify God's higher purpose in the midst of our trials. That's when we must exercise our faith by waiting on His word to us.

A good friend of mine who was a real estate broker experienced a seven-year period of financial failure. The loss of his security devastated him. It became the constant focus of his thoughts and prayers. "Why doesn't God do something?" he would ask me. For a while, we were both puzzled.

But after some intense soul searching, he realized that he had substituted financial security for God in his life. The Father wanted to be recognized as the Source of all things in my friend's life. As he began renewing his mind spiritually and yielding his rights to the Lord, my friend gained a new freedom in his attitude toward finances. He started a new career and found greater financial blessing than ever before.

God had a great and mighty lesson to teach my friend—a lesson more important than keeping him comfortable. And God kept him uncomfortable until he took his eyes off his circumstances and sought God's mind in the matter.

Waiting is not easy. We often turn away from seeking God's counsel and seek guidance from friends and loved ones. We read books, attend seminars, and talk with others, trying to find out what God has to say to us. Usually, after we've exhausted all other possibilities, we turn back to the Lord and wait on Him. By doing this, it's as if we are saying to God, "Now that I've tried everything else and failed, I've decided I need You after all."

But God wants us to come to Him first. He wants us to stand in His counsel and wait for His word. He longs for us to come to Him as a son would to his father. But instead, we go to Him last, as if we don't trust Him or consider His word of much value. Yet He is the only trustworthy Source of counsel we have. He is our most available and accessible Friend. He will never give us a busy signal—even if He frequently gets busy signals when He tries talking to us.

God entreats us to pray because He knows we are often caught in prisons of our own making; not prisons with bars and locks, but intellectual prisons, emotional prisons, and relational prisons. We must remember that the shortest distance between our problems and their solutions is the distance between our knees and the floor.

Answer Promised

Second, God told Jeremiah, "I will answer thee." Sometimes we make commitments that we cannot keep. Though we may do this unintentionally, there are times when we disappoint those who are counting on us. But God never disappoints—when He says He will do something, it will be done.

God promises He will not only hear our prayers, but He will answer them. This brings up two interesting questions: Does God always answer our prayers? Or does He respond to certain kinds of prayer? Think about the requests you have made of God recently. Are they being answered? Do you really believe they will be? You see, the question is not *Does God answer prayer?* The real question is *How does God answer prayer?* Sometimes He answers yes. This is usually the only answer we hear. If God says, "Yes," then we believe He answered. If He says, "No," we think He ignored our request.

God's Answers

When God answers our prayers, He either answers with yes, no, or wait. When He answers yes, we are prone to shout, "Praise the Lord!" We tell everyone what a great thing God has done for us.

But when God says no, we have a hard time finding reasons to praise Him. We look for the sin in our lives that kept Him from granting our requests, because surely if we had been living right He would have given us what we asked. But not one shred of scriptural evidence shows that God will say yes to all of our prayers just because we're living right. God is sovereign. He has the right to say no according to His infinite wisdom, regardless of our goodness.

We try to manipulate God by our humanistic "if then" philosophy. *If* we live good, clean lives, *then* God must (we believe) grant our hearts' desires. But such attempts to manipulate God defeat the whole purpose of Christianity, which is to glorify Him through our submissive obedience to His desires. Besides, if our goodness was the only factor God considered, where would His grace fit in? Many times His grace is what motivates Him to say no.

God only says *no* and *wait* when it is best for us (Rom. 8:28). He does it many times for our protection. Sometimes God *wants* to answer our prayers, but the timing is not right. For example, in the past, many couples wanting to marry came to me for counseling. Sometimes I would advise them to wait. Some would heed my advice, while others sought counsel from those who told them what they wanted to hear. You and I have the same choice over and over again. Will we wait on God for His perfect timing, or will we rush ahead?

We don't like waiting around. Especially when it looks like a unique opportunity might slip away. We don't like to hear God say, "No," especially when everything in us says, "Yes, yes, yes!" We often try to find a Scripture verse and claim it while we continue our prayer, hoping somehow to change God's mind. What we're really saying is, "God, I didn't like that answer. How about reconsidering my point of view?"

But deep in our hearts we really want God's perfect will for our lives. And we must remember that God's answer is always His ultimate best for us. Claiming Scripture will not change God's mind because His Word cannot contradict His will. If He says no, then the answer is no. If He says wait, then we should wait. God is more interested in our character, our future, and our sanctification than He is in our momentary satisfaction. His answers are always an act of grace, motivated by His love.

Our Response

Our response to God's answers reveals one of two things about us. It will reveal either a rebellious spirit or a submissive spirit. By accepting God's answer, despite the fact that we may not understand, we express a submissive spirit. But by refusing His first answer and trying to get our way by manipulation, we express a rebellious spirit.

If we refuse God's answers when they don't fit in with our plans, then we are trying to use God for our purposes. But if we graciously accept His answers—no matter what they are—He will use us for His glory.

The Hidden Revealed

The third principle we can obtain from this verse comes from "I will … show thee great and mighty things, which thou knowest not." All of us face decisions that leave us baffled. We are constantly bombarded with relational decisions, business decisions, household decisions, and financial decisions—and these all need immediate attention. In this verse, God promises to reveal the answer to all of life's decisions. Yet many of God's people spend their entire lives making decisions based on *their* knowledge, *their* understanding, and *their* experience—not realizing that some decisions must be based on divine wisdom and illumination from God.

Almost any preacher can prepare a sermon. He can write an outline, gather a few stories, and away he goes. But a preacher cannot get God's message for a people until he waits in the Lord's counsel, until he seeks God's face, and until God gives him a word from heaven (Jer. 23:21–22).

This same principle applies to every Christian. We can pay the price required to find God's mind on an issue, or we can make a decision based on what *we* think is right. Either way, a decision will eventually be made. But while one decision may have the approval of man, the other will have the eternal approval of God.

Sometimes we flip a coin (spiritually speaking) and say, "Lord, this is what I'm going to do. If it is of You, then bless it. If I'm wrong, then better luck next time." Instead of waiting, we jump ahead and hope we have done the right thing. The point is this: As Christians, we never have to guess—we can know for sure what to do. God wants us to know His will about things, even more than we want to know it. But He cannot—and will not—bless anything we do that is not of Him.

So what does He mean when He says, "I will ... show thee great and mighty things"? Every time we pray to God, seeking His will, there are two things He wants to show us: He wants to show us Himself (Phil. 3:7–8), and He wants to show us what He is able to do (John 15:16). Is there anything greater than seeking God and knowing His power?

We Are to Seek His Face

Because God wants to reveal Himself to us, and because our goal as Christians is to know Him, we should begin our time in prayer saying, "Lord, thank You that You are omnipotent. Thank You that You are omniscient and know everything I am about to tell You. Thank You that You are omnipresent, and You are not separated from me. As I come into Your presence, I humble myself before Your throne to thank You for Your holiness, Your forgiveness, and Your mercy. I acknowledge You as the great Creator,

Sustainer, and Lover of mankind. Father, I am coming to You, recognizing Your greatness and Your holiness. I bow before You as Your child, knowing that You are more than sufficient to meet my needs."

This is the spirit in which we should come into God's presence. But instead, we come first with our needs and usually don't have enough time for anything else. We never stop long enough to recognize that God wants to show us Himself when we pray.

He Shows Us His Power

God also wants to show us what He is able and willing to do for us. He does this through His Word. He reminds us of what He has done in the past. He gives us example after example in Scripture of how He met people's needs and how He protected them. And the Father is willing to do the same thing for us, if we will only ask.

The word *mighty* in this passage means hidden things, things that are fenced in. This word is used when referring to fortified cities. God is showing us that as we pray, He will unveil insights for us that have previously been a mystery.

This also implies that some answers will be found only in prayer, not from other sources—not from books, friends, or counselors. Some things must come straight from God, who is the Source of all wisdom. How many families would still be together today if they had sought God's answers to their problems at home? How many sons and daughters would still be at home if their parents had taken their situation to the Lord? Too often we refuse to wait on God's answers. We want quick solutions to our problems.

But God wants to do much more than just meet our needs and answer our questions. He wants our love. He wants our spirits— He wants our lives. Yes, He encourages us to bring our trials and our heartaches to Him in prayer, but only after we recognize who He is and what He can do. Only then do we believe He will answer our prayers. Only then are we seeking His face and not merely His hand.

As a pastor, many times I go to God for answers that can be found only in Him. Sometimes He shows me something for today, and sometimes He shows me something that will happen in the next week or month. But I've never been to God about anything that He did not willingly answer. He does not always answer my prayers according to *my* time schedule, but He *always* answers on time.

Back in 1969 when I was preaching a weeklong revival meeting in Virginia, I once again felt that God had something specific to say to me. Each night after the service I retired to my room early to pray. One evening, I pulled out a pad and drew a circle with five lines leading from it. At the end of each line, I wrote several things I thought God might desire to reveal to me. On the last line I drew a question mark, thinking maybe it was something I had not thought of.

The following night I came back to my room with the same burden. As I prayed and looked over the possibilities, God made it clear that He was going to move me. I asked Him when, and the month of September flashed into my mind. This happened in May of 1969, but I thought He meant September of 1970. A few months later, however, a pulpit committee from the First Baptist Church of Atlanta came to see me. On September 30, 1969, my family and I moved to Atlanta. God revealed this to me ahead of time in order to prepare my heart. He unveiled what was hidden when I called on Him to do so.

Regardless of what circumstances you are up against, there is no knowledge you will ever need that is not accessible before the throne of our living, loving, holy, righteous God. He has promised to show you the great, the hidden, and the unknown things that you will never be able to understand any other way. There are some things you will never be able to know (Deut. 29:29), but all the knowledge you will ever need is available to you if you ask God.

He desires to illuminate your mind and heart until you are conscious of Christ's mind within you. He wants you to say no to the world on the basis of your faith in Him. It is then that you feel an extra sense of power when you share with others. You no longer depend entirely on circumstances for God to teach you lessons. Instead, you learn straight from Him through His Word. You have a new excitement in your relationship with God because you have learned to listen as He speaks to you.

Submission Required

You must be submissive to God to the point of absolute obedience—regardless of what He asks of you. Why? Because if our heavenly Father continues to answer our prayers, and we have certain conditions on which we obey, then He is nothing more than a giant Santa Claus. If He were to continue to bless us regardless of our rebellion, we would be using Him for our ends, not His. Submission is essential.

If you have been seeking God's will for a long time and you seem to be getting nowhere, examine your heart. See if there is any area of your life that is not totally surrendered to Him. By settling this issue, you will put yourself in a position that will allow the Father to bless you. The quicker you move from your will to His will, the quicker God will show you what you need to know. Since God gives us His Word for obedience, not just consideration, He must be assured that you have submitted yourself completely before He will let you in on His secrets.

Are you facing a decision in your life that is too big for you to handle? Are you going through some difficulty that has left you confused and disheartened? God said, "Call unto me, and I will answer thee, and show thee great and mighty things, which thou knowest not." As you seek God's face, understanding who He is and what He is willing and able to do, He will clear away all the mist that surrounds your circumstances. He will show you what to do. Are you willing to say yes to whatever He requires? If so, you have taken the first step in learning to talk with God.

2
PRAYING WITH AUTHORITY

And it came to pass at the time of the offering of the evening
sacrifice, that Elijah the prophet came near, and said, LORD
God of Abraham, Isaac, and of Israel, let it be known this
day that thou art God in Israel, and that I am thy servant,
and that I have done all these things at thy word. Hear me,
O LORD, hear me, that this people may know that thou art
the LORD God, and that thou hast turned their heart back
again. Then the fire of the LORD fell, and consumed the burnt
sacrifice, and the wood, and the stones, and the dust, and licked
up the water that was in the trench. And when all the people
saw it, they fell on their faces: and they said, The LORD, he is
the God; the LORD, he is the God. —1 Kings 18:36–39

Ahab and Elijah had been enemies for a long time. So Elijah
challenged Ahab and the prophets of Baal to a contest. In essence

he said, "Let's find out whose god is really God. If the god of Baal is God, we should all worship him. If Jehovah is God, then we should all follow Him."

Ahab thought this was fair enough and agreed to go along with Elijah's plan. Elijah instructed him to build an altar and find a suitable sacrifice for his god. Then all the prophets of Baal were to pray and ask their god to consume the offering with fire.

The prophets of Baal prepared their altar and began to pray. They not only prayed, but they also shouted, cried, and cut themselves trying to get their god to prove himself. Finally, Elijah became annoyed with them and started ridiculing them. He teased them and asked, "What's wrong? Is your god asleep? Is he on vacation?" (see 1 Kings 18:27). This stirred them up even more, but still nothing happened.

Elijah decided it was his turn. He rebuilt an old forgotten altar of God and placed his sacrifice on it. Then, to prove his point, he had a barrel of water poured over it. This was repeated twice, until everything was drenched. Satisfied with the altar and sacrifice, Elijah prayed. While everyone watched and listened, Elijah asked God to prove to the entire host that He was the God of Israel. Not only did God consume the sacrifice with fire, but He also consumed the wood, the stones, the dust, and the water as well (1 Kings 18:38). The Lord God had proven Himself.

This is a beautiful demonstration of praying with authority. Elijah didn't hide out in a quiet place, hold a prayer meeting, and tell everyone that God had answered his prayer. If he had, no one would have believed him, and God would not have had the opportunity to prove Himself to the people.

But when Elijah built an altar before the prophets of Baal, soaking it with water, he put himself in a do-or-die situation. Either God had to come through for him, or Elijah would be accused of serving a dead god. With a sense of humility and desperation, Elijah cried out to God—and God answered him with fire from heaven. There was nothing private about Elijah's faith. As a result, God demonstrated His supernatural power publicly. Elijah saw a dream come true when the people said, "The Lord, he is the God." Elijah knew then that he had accomplished his purpose.

Another Example

Many years ago, a certain international missionary organization was having a weeklong conference for their missionaries. This would be the last time many of these missionaries would be able to leave their countries because of an anti-religious stand by their governments.

One missionary from Burma, Ouan Lei, had tried for almost a year to get permission to leave that country. But time after time, his application for a visa was rejected. On the first night of the conference, after all the preliminary introductions were taken care of, one missionary from the United States stood and said he believed that God wanted their friend from Burma to be at the conference.

No one said a word as this older saint began to pray. He began by binding Satan. Then he asked God to change the minds of the officials who were in charge of issuing visas. He prayed for roughly twenty minutes then sat down. After a few additional moments of silence, the conference resumed.

An hour and a half later, a woman from the kitchen came running into the room to announce that someone had just called from Burma and that Ouan Lei had received permission to leave the country. Like Elijah, that saint from the United States knew how to pray with the kind of authority that moves God.

Claiming God's Promises

Think of all the promises God has given in Scripture regarding answered prayer. How many of these promises do we claim on a daily basis? More often than not, we complain about our needs and our problems. We tiptoe around the throne room of God, afraid to ask Him for what we really want. We don't go to Him on the basis of what He said He would do—we go weakly and fearfully.

But according to Scripture, we are to approach Him boldly with our prayers (Heb. 4:16). When we leave our place of prayer, we should be expecting God's answer. God doesn't want us walking around with attitudes of fear and doubt, wondering if He will do anything about our requests. He has given us a spirit of power, not one of timidity or fear (2 Tim. 1:7).

"For we have not an high priest which cannot be touched with the feeling of our infirmities; but was in all points tempted like as we are, yet without sin. Let us therefore come boldly unto the throne of grace, that we may obtain mercy, and find grace to help in time of need" (Heb. 4:15–16). Christ is our go-between to the Father. We get to God on the basis of Christ's righteousness, not our own.

Therefore, we can go to God the Father with the same authority that Christ Jesus did. This is the reason we can go to God boldly and with a sense of authority. Because of our position in Christ, we can pray with authority, believing that God will honor our prayers.

Jehoshaphat's Example

Let's look at another good example of praying with authority. Jehoshaphat had just heard the news that a great multitude was coming against him from beyond the seas to take the people of God into captivity. Scripture says Jehoshaphat was afraid and called for fasting and prayer throughout the nation. In desperation and fear, he cried out to the Lord. In essence he prayed, "O God of heaven, is it not You who is Master over all the nations in the earth? We have no might. We have no strength. All we can do is focus our attention on You" (see 2 Chron. 20:6–12). God heard Jehoshaphat's prayer and caused his enemies to destroy themselves.

Elijah and Jehoshaphat are two clear examples of men who approached God fearlessly, boldly, and courageously, making petitions that would allow God to glorify Himself. But how often do we go to God concentrating on our own sense of inability and helplessness? We say, "Oh, Lord, You know my needs. I hope You will do something about them." That is not praying with authority, but with defeat.

God's Power and Authority in Us

Praying with authority doesn't mean we go to God proudly, demanding our way in spite of His will. The concept of authority means something entirely different. Christ said, "All power is given unto me in heaven and in earth" (Matt. 28:18). The Greek word used here for power (*exousia*) means that Christ had the power and freedom to do anything He pleased with no hindrances. He had unlimited power and unlimited freedom to use it.

"But ye shall receive power, after that the Holy Ghost is come upon you" (Acts 1:8). The word used in this verse comes from a different Greek word (*dynamis*). It means having the supernatural capacity of God to bring forth something in the name of Jesus Christ. Christ had God's power in an unlimited capacity, whereas we have God's power in conjunction with accomplishing His will. So when Christ sent the disciples out (Matt. 28), they went with the confidence that they would be granted all the power they needed. Since Christ had all the power in heaven and earth, He could give them that same power.

Both types of power are mentioned in Luke 9:1. "Then [Jesus] called his twelve disciples together, and gave them power [*dynamis*] and authority [*exousia*] over all devils, and to cure diseases." God gave them the divine capacity to execute His will. At this point in their ministry, they received the ability to bring forth what God had commissioned them to do. But having the ability was not enough. They had to have the authority (or the right) to claim their position of power over all demons and illnesses; Christ gave them that right.

When God gives us a commission, He always equips us for the job. He has made provision for our needs before the needs ever arise. Our problem is that we don't apply the power and authority

He has made available to us. As a result, we come up answerless and frustrated in our prayer lives. This will continue until we do God's work in God's power—not our own.

God has placed in the hands of every believer the most miraculous and supernatural power this world will ever know. Yet we still live powerless lives, pray powerless prayers, and do powerless works. As a result, the church is weak. And because the church is weak, nations are weak. We will never accomplish what God wants accomplished as a body—or as individuals—until we learn to go to Him, claiming the power and authority He has granted us ... a power and authority that gives us the right and ability to do the works of God.

This authority does not give us license to make demands of God. By studying the prayers of Elijah and Jehoshaphat, we see that they went to God with a deep sense of humility. They went with boldness, but not with pride. Humility is essential if we desire to pray with authority. Humility means agreeing with God about who we are and what we can do. Humility eliminates the idea that we tell God what to do. In actuality, we are crying out in desperation for Him to intervene in our circumstances.

Praying with authority is essential if we are to pray effective prayers that free God to work. Praying without authority lacks urgency, which allows Satan to sidetrack us. Without urgency, we lose heart in our prayers. The least little thing becomes an excuse to quit. Without a sense of urgency, our minds are easily divided. How many times have you found yourself saying empty words that you felt went no higher than the ceiling? Lack of urgency in prayer gives Satan the foothold he needs to completely demoralize and despiritualize our prayer lives.

Prayer—Our Spiritual Battlefield

Why does Satan put such a high priority on destroying our prayer lives? Paul wrote, "For we wrestle not against flesh and blood, but against principalities, against powers, against the rulers of the darkness of this world, against spiritual wickedness in high places" (Eph. 6:12). As Christians, we are in a spiritual battle. The only time Satan worries about us is when we enter into this battle. Nothing else we do is much of a threat. Satan knows that real spiritual battle is fought on our knees. Prayer is the weapon he fears most; therefore, it is prayer against which he makes his greatest attack. It is on our knees that the greatest good is done, and it is on our knees that we will face our greatest assaults.

There was a period in my life when every time I knelt to pray, I would fall asleep. Regardless of how much sleep I had, I could not stay awake when I began to pray. I did everything I knew to do, but nothing helped. I had no problem studying, even when I arose early, but I couldn't pray ten minutes without falling asleep.

I struggled with this for almost a year until the Lord revealed the problem to me. Satan would rather I preach or study than pray. He would rather I do *anything* but pray. To hinder me, he attacked me with a spirit of slumber. When I realized this, I asked God to tear down this stronghold of slumber and to replace it with a spirit of alertness. The problem immediately disappeared. The joy of my prayer life was revived, the struggle with slumber ceased, and once again I entered into the heat of the battle.

Paul tells the believer how to prepare for this spiritual battle (Eph. 6:13–17). He makes it clear that *all* the armor is essential if we are to stand firm. Paul knew that prayer was much more than rushing to God and making a few quick requests. He saw it as a battle, and we must see it that way too. It is in prayer that our battles are won and lost. Therefore, it is essential that we learn how to pray.

Satan not only attacks our concentration in prayer, but he attacks our faith as well. As long as we pray without authority, doubts can slip in. Our enemy will do everything in his power to increase our doubts and destroy our faith.

It is these doubts that Satan uses against us by saying things like, "You can't ask God for that. Who do you think you are? You are just a sinner. What makes you think you can bother a holy God with your little problems?"

The issue is that without any authority in our prayers, we cannot rebuke the enemy and bind him from our thoughts. In the same way, the church is powerless against Satan's attacks unless it gets the power and authority of God back into its prayers. Satan would love for the church to continue in the direction it's been going in past generations, coming timidly to the gates of hell with no prevailing power whatsoever. But this is our own fault. We attempt to fight this battle in the flesh, not in the spirit. We're fighting a spiritual battle without spiritual power, and we're losing.

Satan is not concerned with how many times we go to church or how many hymns we sing. He does not feel threatened by our organizations or our cutting-edge technologies. But when God's people fall on their knees and claim Christ's power and authority, everything in heaven will begin to move, and everything in hell will begin to shake.

There are five prerequisites if we are to go to God with a sense of authority.

Our Relationship

First, we must have a genuine personal relationship with God through His Son, Jesus Christ. Since our authority is based on our position in Christ, we must be in Him to receive His authority. Salvation is the first step.

God's Thoughts

Second, we must know God's thoughts (1 Cor. 2:11–12). This is one of the main reasons God has given us His Word. The Bible shows us God's thoughts in our vocabulary. The more we saturate our minds with Scripture, the more like God we will think. His view of things will become our view. His attitudes will become our attitudes.

As a result, it becomes easier for us to know His will—and knowing His will is essential if we are to pray with authority. Why? Because if we know we are praying in agreement with God about something, we also know it is just a matter of time until He brings it about. Knowing His will in our prayers gives us the confidence that He is on our side.

Sometimes we run into questions that don't seem to be answered in Scripture. Some circumstances and problems seem so unique that we may not even look to Scripture for an answer. We feel the need to go to another source. But we must remember, there are no unique problems. Somewhere, someone has run into a similar situation as yours, or one where the same principles are involved. In Scripture, God has provided us with basic principles for handling any circumstance we face. But it is up to us to search the Bible to find out what His Word says.

Another way God speaks to us is through the prayers of biblical characters. Find a prayer that goes along with your particular problem or need, and put the prayer in your own words. Then, search Scripture to find how God answered that prayer in the life of the one who prayed it. It may be a prayer for wisdom as Solomon prayed, or a cry for help as in Jehoshaphat's case. But remember that the same God who met the needs of men and women during biblical times is able to meet your needs today.

The key is to pray according to God's will. To know His will, we must know His thoughts. To know His thoughts, we must saturate our minds with His Word. Then we will begin to experience the authority of God in our prayers.

Pure Heart

Third, we must have pure hearts if we are to pray with authority. There can be no known sin in our lives. Sin means a divided loyalty. God will not trust His authority and power to anyone who is not completely yielded to His purpose. Therefore, when we *do* sin, we must confess and repent—not just so we can get God's power back, but out of a genuine spirit of sorrow and grief over our sin.

One afternoon a woman and her husband came to see me for marriage counseling. As they described their problems, it became evident that the wife was suffering from satanic oppression. I told them what I thought their problem was and asked for permission to pray for the wife's deliverance and protection. They both quickly agreed, and so we prayed.

Three days later the husband called and told me things were worse than before. There seemed to be no change in his wife, and they were both discouraged. This troubled me greatly. *Why didn't God answer my prayer?* I thought. As I began to meditate on Scripture, God brought to my mind an area of disobedience that I had not dealt with. I realized that this sin had negated my power and authority to bind Satan from the woman's life. I made things right with the Lord and called the couple back to set up another counseling session.

When they came, we prayed again. This time a miraculous change took place. The woman's erratic behavior stopped immediately, her oppression lifted, her countenance changed, and her fellowship with her husband was restored. But it wasn't until I dealt with my own life that God was free to work in hers.

Satan will often try to use sin against us when we pray. This is why we shouldn't dwell on our sins once they have been confessed. Satan wants us walking around feeling guilty and unworthy. But it is the righteousness of Christ that allows us entry to the Father. It is a righteousness that comes from God on the basis of faith (Phil. 3:9). So once sin has been properly dealt with, we should forget it.

Pure Motives

Fourth, we need pure motives if we are to pray with authority. Remember what Elijah said? "Lord, You know why I did this. I am Your servant and I have done all these things at Your word." When we go to the heavenly Father, we must know in our hearts that our motives are pure. We must pray according to God's will, not according to our own selfish desires clothed in inappropriate Scripture.

However, not *every* personal request is selfish. The key is to have committed our lives to God before we start praying. If we have done so, we will want God's will more than the particular thing for which we are asking. When God knows we want His purpose accomplished more than we want anything else, He can trust us with His power. But as long as we pray with selfish motives, we cannot be trusted.

A Persistent Confidence

Finally, we must have a persistent confidence in the faithfulness of God. This means that the consistency of His Word will be reflected in the consistency of our prayers. We must pray until we see an answer. If we really believe we are praying according to God's will, then why should we stop praying before we see an answer? Many times we pray fervently for a while, then we lose interest and say, "Well, I guess it wasn't God's will." This is an excuse for our lack of importunity. But if we are to pray with authority, we must continue in the battle until we see victory.

Praying with authority is a basic truth that must be applied if we are to learn to talk with God effectively. It is a matter of claiming that which has already been bought and paid for by Christ at Calvary. When we pray with the authority God has given us, we will see our prayers become the effective tools they were meant to be. Our lives and the lives of those around us will be changed. His authority has been promised. Now we must decide whether or not to pay the price necessary to make it part of our lives.

3

PRAYING AND FASTING

Take heed that ye do not your alms before men, to be seen of them:
otherwise ye have no reward of your Father which is in heaven....
And when thou prayest, thou shalt not be as the hypocrites are: for
they love to pray standing in the synagogues and in the corners
of the streets, that they may be seen of men. Verily I say unto you,
They have their reward.... Moreover when ye fast, be not, as the
hypocrites, of a sad countenance: for they disfigure their faces,
that they may appear unto men to fast. Verily I say unto you, They
have their reward. But thou, when thou fastest, anoint thine head,
and wash thy face, That thou appear not unto men to fast, but
unto thy Father which is in secret: and thy Father, which seeth
in secret, shall reward thee openly. —Matthew 6:1, 5, 16–18

At the start of my third year in seminary, the pulpit committee of
a little church in North Carolina extended a call to me to be their

pastor. I was also offered a teaching position at a Bible institute near the church. The church would allow me to teach in the institute while serving as pastor.

However, I had never been a pastor. While my feelings were mixed, the overwhelming emotions were fear and inadequacy. As I prayed about and pondered the opportunity, my list of negatives grew every day. The congregation would have to wait seven months for me, and by then they may have found someone else they liked better.

I was totally ignorant of the real problems facing a pastor. Besides, I felt that the pastors who studied at the Bible institute wouldn't listen to an inexperienced seminary graduate teach them homiletics (sermon preparation), preaching (sermon delivery), and evangelism.

Back and forth I went: *No, it can't be God's will. Yes, it must be of Him—I didn't ask for this.* For several weeks my faith wavered. I was growing mentally, emotionally, and physically weary. I couldn't find clear direction from the Lord.

Then one morning I was reading from the book of Daniel. As I began chapter 9, hope swelled within me. I knew I had found a way to know God's will—and to know for sure. If God honored Daniel's fasting, why wouldn't He honor mine?

I had never fasted before. As I look back, I realize that I had never felt the need. But I was desperate then for God's clear direction regarding the opportunities offered to me.

After three days of fasting, confessing, listening, and searching the Word of God, I felt clean, pruned, filled, and confident that the call was God's assignment. I would go with the assurance of His divine assistance.

In June of the following year, my family and I moved to Fruitland, North Carolina, to an exciting ministry that will always be one of the highlights of my life. Why? It was the call to that ministry which revealed my need to practice the biblical principles of fasting.

History

Throughout history, a new thirst for God has always awakened a renewed interest in fasting. It was true of Old Testament saints such as Moses the lawgiver, David the king, Elijah the prophet, and Daniel the seer.

Reformers such as John Calvin, Martin Luther, and John Knox practiced fasting. So did revivalists like Jonathan Edwards, John Wesley, and Charles G. Finney.

Evidence exists today that a new thirst for the Spirit is once again beginning to awaken the slumbering church. And once again there is a growing interest in the practice of fasting.

Fasting Defined

First, let's define the term *fasting*. It is more than mere self-denial or abstinence, but it does involve both. It is abstinence with a spiritual goal in mind. Fasting is abstinence from anything that hinders our communion with God.

According to Scripture, fasting can take several forms. First, there is the food fast, which means abstaining from all food, illustrated by Christ's fast following His baptism (Luke 4:2). Second is the absolute fast, which means abstaining from drinking as well as eating. This is illustrated by Ezra's fast as he mourned over the faithlessness of the people of God in exile (Ezra 10:6). A third form of fasting involves the mutual consent of marriage partners to abstain from sexual relations. This is the implication of Paul's exhortation to the married (1 Cor. 7:3–6).

In Matthew 6, Christ talks about praying, giving, and fasting (vv. 1–18). He stresses that we check our motives. We must ask ourselves, *Why am I doing this?* We are not to do these things to be seen by others. We are to pray in secret, not in public like the hypocrites. We are to give in such a way that no one knows how much we give. And when we fast, it should be kept between us and the Lord.

Prayer, giving, and fasting are private acts of worship, and therefore should be done privately. We should do them out of love for God, not because we crave the world's praise. If we do these things for the praise of the world, then the world's praise will be all the blessing we receive.

Christ did not say that our witness should be kept to ourselves, but rather certain forms of worship—in this case prayer, fasting, and giving. This will keep us from becoming proud and comparing ourselves with other Christians.

Throughout Scripture, references are made to fasting as an aid to prayer. Before Moses received the Ten Commandments, he fasted and prayed (Ex. 34:28). David fasted to deepen his own relationship with the Father (Ps. 69:10). When the nation of Israel was being attacked, the leaders would often call the people to fast and pray, asking God to intervene on their behalf (2 Chron. 20:3). Daniel spent a prolonged period fasting and praying to discern God's timetable concerning Israel's return to Jerusalem from Babylonian captivity (Dan. 9:3). After hearing God's warning through Jonah, the nation of Nineveh began to fast and pray, and God withheld His judgment (Jonah 3:5).

Jesus spent the first forty days after His baptism fasting and praying, seeking the mind of His Father (Luke 4:1–2). When the New Testament church began, the believers fasted and prayed. Before Paul and Barnabas were sent out, they fasted and prayed (Acts 13:2–3).

Throughout the Bible, God directed His people to fast and pray. And every time people fasted and prayed, God released His supernatural power to bring about whatever was necessary to meet their needs. Whether it was wisdom or the defeat of an enemy, God was always faithful to provide.

Since God so mightily honored the prayers of men and women in the Bible who fasted, we should make fasting a part of our lives as well. But there are four principles we must understand if we are going to effectively combine the tool of fasting with our prayers.

Obedience

First of all, fasting does not negate our responsibility to be obedient to God. We cannot fast and pray and expect God to bless us when there is known sin in our lives. Fasting does not impress God with our spirituality to the point that He ignores our sin. On the contrary, genuine fasting will always cause us to examine our hearts to make sure everything is right with Him.

If God exposes some sin in our lives while we're fasting, we must deal with it in whatever manner He requires. This may mean interrupting our prayer time so that we can make things right with someone we have offended, or it may mean a commitment to make restitution at a later date. The point is that fasting may be used by God to *expose* sin, but we cannot use it to *cover up* sin.

The Control of Appetites

The second principle is that fasting brings our physical appetites under the Holy Spirit's control. We all have appetites or drives. Each of us has a hunger drive, sex drive, emotional drive, approval drive, and many more. God has given us these drives to be fulfilled within the boundaries of His Word. There are times, however, when we are to set aside the fulfilling of these drives so that we may seek Him with our whole hearts. As we do this, we reach the point when our greatest desire will be undisturbed communion with the Father. We are able to talk with Him more honestly and listen to Him more attentively.

These appetites and drives are not evil, though they are often thought to be. They are gifts from God. But if abused, they can become curses. That is why they must be kept in subjection to our desire for God. These drives were given to us in order that they may serve us. But when they get out of balance, we become their slaves. By fasting, we can restore the balance God originally intended.

As a pastor, I counsel many people who are slaves to their drives. The most common problem is in the area of sexual lust. "I'm trapped. I can't help myself. Please help me. I'm afraid of what I might do." These are the cries of sincere believers caught in the web of a desire out of control—lust.

It often requires more than reading the Bible to be freed from such bondage. Thought patterns must be changed. The mind must be renewed (Rom. 12:1–2). The sex drive has to be brought under the authority of the Holy Spirit. Fasting is a divine aid in bringing about this change.

One afternoon a young man came into my office weeping. He told me about his long and futile battle against lust. He had tried everything he knew to get victory, but nothing worked.

As we talked, I challenged him to fast for three days. I told him to seclude himself and spend his time in two activities. First, he was to pray—not, "Oh, Lord, please help me," but rather praising God and thanking Him for the victory he was gaining moment by moment. His prayers were to be positive.

Second, he was to fill his mind with Scripture. He was to read passages that dealt specifically with his problem (1 Thess. 4:1–7; Gal. 5:16–18; Col. 3:5). He was also to meditate on passages that assured him of God's presence and power in his life (Ps. 57:1–2). Then I challenged him to fast one day each week for the three weeks following. After that, I told him we would talk again.

One month later he returned. Fasting had really been a struggle for him, especially the first day. "I was tempted to give up every hour," he said, "but by the evening of the second day, I knew victory was possible." During this time he said he experienced total freedom from lust, though the temptations never ceased.

This young man walked out of my office free. He decided to continue fasting one day a week, however, as a reminder of what God had done for him. His prayers would now naturally be full of praise and thanksgiving, for God had delivered him from bondage.

Could one or two drives in your life be out of balance? Sometimes you might win the fight, while other times you might lose. This situation does not have to exist. You can have complete victory if you will allow God to help you put all your drives under the Holy Spirit's control. When this happens, you'll find freedom that you never thought was possible.

Control of the Holy Spirit

A third principle is that fasting helps bring our minds, wills, and emotions under the Holy Spirit's control. Fasting allows us to think clearly and quickly. As a result, there is a new and constant awareness of God's presence during times of fasting. His presence becomes more evident, even in the midst of our daily routine. During times of fasting, our minds are quicker to discern the things of the Spirit. This is especially important when we're seeking guidance for a big decision.

Aids in Worship

A fourth principle is that fasting is a tremendous aid when we seek the Lord in worship. What would happen if you and I began to fast on Saturdays before we went to the Lord's house on Sunday?

What would happen if an entire congregation did this? The worship service would become a *real* worship service. When people begin to fast, pray, and seek God—and He becomes the priority of their thinking, feeling, and action—something begins to happen to them and everyone around them.

When Jesus spoke about fasting, He didn't say *if* you fast—but *when* you fast. What reasons do we find in Scripture for fasting?

Disciplines Our Spirits

Fasting disciplines our spirits toward the things of the Father. When the time came for Jesus to seek direction concerning His ministry, He spent time fasting and praying. For forty days and nights He disciplined His spirit and body in order to find His Father's will. Though Christ was closer to God than anyone on earth, He still found it necessary to go this extra mile.

He knew that fasting brings one's relationship with God to a point that it becomes an absolute priority. Fasting allows us to discipline ourselves, and therefore places us in a position whereby we can reach our maximum potential both mentally and spiritually.

Many Christians don't see the necessity of fasting. But if Christ found it necessary, then it is necessary for us, too. If we are to reach our maximum potential, we must know what God has to say to us individually. This calls for intense prayer. Fasting intensifies prayer, allowing us to reach into the innermost part of our spirits until we can understand spiritual things that we otherwise could not grasp.

How many times have we said or heard others say, "I just don't know what I'm feeling. I can't seem to figure it out"? Fasting prunes and peels off layer after layer of feelings, attitudes, and experiences until we get to the hard core of what God desires to say to us. Fasting is the discipline of the spirit.

Finding God's Will

Fasting helps us find God's will. For example, let's say you are contemplating marriage. You don't really know for sure that this is God's will, but you think it might be. You've prayed, read, and talked to counselors, but you still aren't sure.

Here is a suggestion: Spend three days alone on your face before God, fasting and praying for guidance. Tell Him that you want Him to show you through His Word what you should do. God honors this kind of praying. As you fast and pray, He will clear your eyes, your ears, your heart, and your spirit. Your attention will be turned toward Him, and you will hear from God as never before. His leading will become clear, and you will be able to follow His plans with complete assurance of His blessings.

Daniel understood this principle. He struggled over a prophecy of Jeremiah. He knew there was something God wanted him to know, but it just would not come clear. So he fasted and prayed before the Lord. He gave up the fulfilling of certain physical appetites in order to find out what God was saying.

We need to ask ourselves: *Do I want to reach my potential for God, or am I willing to be satisfied with just getting by spiritually? Do I desire the applause and praise of others more than the praise of God? Do I want to fulfill my appetites, or do I want to fulfill God's will?*

If we look at our daily schedules, we'll see that we are consumed with fulfilling our fleshly appetites rather than our spiritual
ones. Then we turn right around and complain that God doesn't
speak to us. He seems so far away. If we expect God to reveal His
direction and will for our lives, we must put Him first. This often
means putting aside the fulfillment of our physical appetites so
that we can focus our attention on Him.

Aids in Repentance

Fasting is often associated with personal repentance and confession.
For example, let's say you have a habit that you cannot overcome.
You know there is a truth that will set you free, but somehow you just
cannot find it. You've tried everything, yet you still have no victory.

So you begin to fast. At first it is a struggle, as Satan attacks
with everything he knows is effective against you. He says, "Do
you really think this is going to work? What is your family going
to think? And besides, you aren't supposed to tell anyone, but they
already know. You're just wasting your time."

On and on he goes, up until the moment God reveals to you
how to be free. All fasting will not be this tough. But remember the
closer you get to victory the harder Satan will work to discourage you.

If you have ever tried to fast and pray and have failed to be
true to your commitment, then you've experienced such attacks.
But often we don't recognize our enemy. We become full of self-
condemnation, when actually we should be encouraged that Satan
is worried enough to even bother with us. Satan knows when one
of God's children repents with fasting and prayer, He will cleanse

that child and remove the strongholds. He knows that when we go to God in this way, we'll see ourselves in a new light. We'll see sin, wickedness, and carnality in our hearts we have never seen before. Therefore, Satan will do anything he can to keep us from getting too serious about repenting and confessing.

There is no incident in the Bible of people fasting, praying, and repenting when God did not release His supernatural power in their lives. The same holds true today. If the body of Christ fasted and prayed one day each week, God's power would be released in a way we have never seen before. Churches would be filled. People would be in no hurry to leave the services. Through our confession and repentance, we would free God to send the revival this world needs so desperately.

Fasting is not necessary every time we confess sin, but it serves as an outward sign of genuine sorrow and grief over sin. It shows God that we are more concerned about correcting our relationship with Him than we are fulfilling our fleshly appetites.

Are you at the point in your life where you say, "I want to be everything God wants me to be, but I just cannot seem to get things straight"? Do you feel as if there is something holding you back? Then I challenge you to spend a day alone with God, fasting and praying. Tell your family what your plans are without making a big deal out of it.

If you are having some sort of family problem, it may be a good idea to fast and pray with your spouse. You may even want to include your entire family. Either way, God will do something supernatural in your life and in your family's life.

Protection of a Nation

The Bible mentions fasting for the protection of a nation regularly. In 2 Chronicles 20, Jehoshaphat called the nation of Israel to fast after he heard that an enemy was approaching. In desperation he fell on his face and cried out to God before the people. When he finished, God spoke through a prophet who was standing in the congregation.

The Lord told Jehoshaphat to get his army together and march into battle—with the choir and orchestra leading the way. Now you can imagine how amazed the enemy was when the choir came out first—so amazed that they became confused. God defeated them, but He did not do it the natural or normal way.

We would like to see God save our nations by sending a great spiritual awakening, but we don't know what God's plans are. We do, however, know that God honors fasting and praying on behalf of nations. If we get concerned and burdened enough, no one will have to beg us to fast. It will be no effort at all.

My concern is this: How far must we go as nations before Christians finally wake up and see what is happening? How far must we go before we fast and pray regularly for God's deliverance? I believe He is waiting on us. But like Jehoshaphat, we must recognize our danger and our weaknesses, and then recognize our Deliverer.

Accomplishing God's Work

Fasting is also mentioned in Scripture in relation to people's concern for accomplishing God's work. Look at Nehemiah's example.

When he was serving as the king's cupbearer, he heard news that Jerusalem's walls were broken down and that the gates were burned. He wrote, "And it came to pass, when I heard these words, that I sat down and wept, and mourned certain days, and fasted, and prayed before the God of heaven" (Neh. 1:4). Verses 5 through 11 continue with the record of Nehemiah's prayer. He fasted and prayed while keeping his burden to himself.

One day the king asked Nehemiah, "Why is thy countenance sad?" (Neh. 2:2). Then Nehemiah became afraid, for it was improper to show grief in the king's presence. People were supposed to be cheerful to keep the king in a good mood.

But Nehemiah's grief was too much to keep inside, so he told the king about his people and their desperate condition. He described the condition of the city and the walls. Then the heathen king asked how he could help Nehemiah. Though taken by surprise at his offer, Nehemiah told how he wanted to return to Jerusalem to rebuild the walls.

The king was faithful to his word, and he let Nehemiah return to Jerusalem. Along with him he sent all the supplies needed to repair the walls and the gates. Then, to top it all off, he sent an escort from his own army to guard Nehemiah.

This is a perfect illustration of what happens when God's people fast and pray over a concern for God's work. Today, however, we often try to do God's work in our own strength. We use the world's resources to finance God's work and the world's principles to maintain His work. But God cautions us not to be conformed to the world's ways of doing things. Rather, we are to use His principles.

What if Nehemiah had tried to work out a way to rebuild the walls without waiting on God? Where could a slave have gotten that much money? How could he have left the city without being caught? And even if he had gotten that far, he would have risked being recaptured and put in prison. In other words, God's work would have never been done—not through Nehemiah, anyway.

I wonder how much of God's work never gets done or is delayed as a result of our wrong thinking. As we do God's work in God's way, we do it in God's power. In His power the impossible becomes reality. We are merely instruments to be used for His glory.

God wants us to be occupied with the salvation of souls, for it is every Christian's responsibility. The church of the Lord Jesus Christ is larger and richer than it has ever been before. Yet we are falling further and further behind in our calling to fulfill the Great Commission. Why? Because somewhere along the way we lost our dependence on the Holy Spirit, and we have tried to win the world through clever mottos, persuasive speeches, manipulated emotions, and useless gimmicks.

But it isn't working.

Spiritual Awakening

I believe God wants to send a spiritual awakening to every nation, but He will not send it until He knows we are ready. We must quit trusting in our own strength and resources, and start pleading with God through fasting and prayer to send us His anointing. Only then will we be prepared to do His work—and only then will God send revival to the world.

But we aren't desperate enough yet. We still have the idea that we can have a revival without making too much of a personal sacrifice. As individuals and as the body of Christ, we need to confess and repent of this attitude of pride. Such self-sufficiency keeps God from accomplishing His work through us.

Before a recent election, our church members set aside a period of ten days to fast and pray. The idea was to have someone fasting and praying twenty-four hours a day during the entire ten-day period. One couple misunderstood the announcement and thought they were supposed to fast all ten days—so they did! When they found out their mistake, they came to tell me what had happened. They were beaming. Both said it was the greatest experience of their lives. They said God used that time to point out some hidden sins in their personal lives that had been affecting their marriage. He cleansed their lives and restored their relationship with each other. They were excited about trying it again.

God wants to do a supernatural work in your life and in the life of your family. He wants you to have His best. It is my prayer that you will allow God to exercise His power through your life in the way He sees fit. Most likely, it will mean making some kind of sacrifice—perhaps through prayer and fasting. But is there any price too great when we consider what Christ did for us?

4

A PRAYER BURDEN

The words of Nehemiah the son of Hachaliah. And it came to pass in the month Chisleu, in the twentieth year, as I was in Shushan the palace, That Hanani, one of my brethren, came, he and certain men of Judah; and I asked them concerning the Jews that had escaped, which were left of the captivity, and concerning Jerusalem. And they said unto me, The remnant that are left of the captivity there in the province are in great affliction and reproach: the wall of Jerusalem also is broken down, and the gates thereof are burned with fire. And it came to pass, when I heard these words, that I sat down and wept, and mourned certain days, and fasted, and prayed before the God of heaven, And said, I beseech thee, O LORD God of heaven, the great and terrible God, that keepeth covenant and mercy for them that love him and observe his commandments: Let thine ear now be attentive, and thine eyes open, that thou mayest hear the prayer of thy servant, which I pray before thee

now, day and night, for the children of Israel thy servants,
and confess the sins of the children of Israel, which we have
sinned against thee: both I and my father's house have sinned.
We have dealt very corruptly against thee, and have not kept
the commandments, nor the statutes, nor the judgments, which
thou commandedst thy servant Moses. Remember, I beseech thee,
the word that thou commandedst thy servant Moses, saying,
If ye transgress, I will scatter you abroad among the nations:
But if ye turn unto me, and keep my commandments, and do
them; though there were of you cast out unto the uttermost
part of the heaven, yet will I gather them from thence, and
will bring them unto the place that I have chosen to set my
name there. Now these are thy servants and thy people, whom
thou hast redeemed by thy great power, and by thy strong
hand. O LORD, *I beseech thee, let now thine ear be attentive*
to the prayer of thy servant, and to the prayer of thy servants,
who desire to fear thy name: and prosper, I pray thee, thy
servant this day, and grant him mercy in the sight of this
man. For I was the king's cupbearer. —Nehemiah 1:1–11

My friend Jack, who was pastoring a church in Miami at the time, told me this story:

One Monday afternoon around 4:00, a woman in Jack's congregation was preparing dinner when she suddenly became concerned about him. She tried to put him out of her mind, but for some reason she couldn't stop thinking about him.

She left the kitchen, went into her bedroom, and began praying. As she prayed, she began crying. She pleaded with God to sustain Jack in this crisis, whatever it was. This went on for thirty minutes. Then, as suddenly as it came, the burden left her. She went back to cooking and didn't think about it again until the next Sunday when she saw Jack at church.

She told Jack what had happened and asked him if anything was wrong. With a look of amazement, he shared his harrowing experience.

On that same Monday, he was flying his private single-engine plane from Miami to Ft. Pierce, Florida. Being in a hurry, he failed to check his fuel.

About halfway to Ft. Pierce, the plane's engine began to sputter and finally quit. He looked at his watch—it was 4:00 p.m. As the plane was losing altitude, Jack started praying and looking for a place to land. But there was no suitable place in sight.

As he prepared for a crash landing, Jack spotted a field that had just been plowed and cleared for planting. By that time his aircraft was losing altitude rapidly, and the field was still a long way off. He knew the outcome of this situation was totally in the Lord's hands.

Jack made it to the field. When his plane finally came to a halt, the nose cone was resting gently against a tree. Neither Jack nor his plane was damaged in any way. As Jack thanked God for saving him, he looked at his watch—it was 4:30.

As Jack concluded his account of the previous Monday, both he and the woman had tears in their eyes. She had been an instrument of God in a crisis. He had been the focus of God's love and watchful care. Together they were an example of how God uses prayer burdens to care for those He loves.

Praying with a burden is probably the most neglected aspect of prayer. As a result, we often pray burdenless prayers. We repeat the same old requests over and over, but with no heart or sense of urgency.

To illustrate the principle of praying with a burden, we return to the story of Nehemiah. Nehemiah was a slave in Babylon, serving as cupbearer to the king. Everything was going along fine until some of his friends from Jerusalem went to Babylon and told him about the awful condition of the city. He became burdened then wept and mourned.

The Source of a Burden

According to Scripture, burdens come from one of three sources. Sometimes we feel burdened as a result of *unconfessed sin*. The way to handle this is simply to confess the sin and move on. Sometimes we feel burdened because of *negative attitudes*. These attitudes can be ours or they can be attitudes that someone else has toward us. Either way, wrong thinking can become an unnecessary burden, one that will eventually lead to ruin.

At other times *God* gives us a burden. A burden from the Lord is a heaviness of heart and spirit. It is an expression of His concern regarding sin in a person's life or a particular need this individual may have. The burden's main function is to get us on our knees before the Father, praying in accordance with His will.

There are several aspects of a prayer burden that we must understand if we are to recognize a burden from the Lord and respond to it properly. Once we get these key principles rooted in our minds, we will see lasting fruit as a result of our God-given burdens.

A burden from the Father is always directed toward a specific need—toward something or someone He wants to change. The burden may be in response to sin in the life of the one with the burden, or it may be in response to sin in the life of a friend. In Nehemiah's case, he was burdened as a result of God's sorrow over the sad state of affairs in Jerusalem. God wanted those circumstances changed, and He burdened Nehemiah.

Evidence of God's Intentions

When God burdens our hearts to pray, He intends to do something about that for which He has burdened us. If the Lord burdens your heart about someone who is lost, this is evidence that He plans to save that person. Often God will use the person He burdens to help accomplish His will. If He burdens you to pray for someone who has a financial need, He probably wants you to help meet that need in a material way, as well as through prayer.

It is important to remember that prayer always begins with God. For instance, let's say God sees you have a need. He begins searching for someone who is available to receive the burden. He may choose someone who is a close friend or someone you hardly know. Either way, He looks for someone who is living an obedient, godly life—someone He can trust to follow through once the prayer burden is received.

Once God finds someone and gives the burden, that person begins to have a heavy heart for you. The Father then will increase the burden and its intensity until it becomes very real and that person understands the importance of his sensitivity to God's will. This individual begins to intercede on your behalf as the Lord leads. God is then free to work on behalf of his prayers, and He meets your need. It may be met through the person praying or through some other means.

How It Works

In essence, this process works like a triangle: God burdens person A; person A prays for person B; person B has his need met by God; and person A is blessed by seeing an answer to prayer. Often when God meets our needs, we get the impression that it was a result of our prayers only. But we never know whom God has burdened for us. When we get to heaven and see who was praying for us and *when* they were praying for us, we will be both surprised and humbled. None of us are sufficient in ourselves—we need the prayers of each other.

But why should an omnipotent God use this triangle of prayer to accomplish His will? He can answer prayers without outside help, can't He? If the Father sees my need, why should He bother anyone else with it?

Sure, God doesn't need us to accomplish His will. But He has chosen this method to allow us to be blessed by seeing Him work in others' lives. He wants us involved with one another on a spiritual basis—loving and encouraging one another. God uses this triangle of prayer to unify us. He allows us to be part of someone else's blessing by involving us in the answer to the prayer. This is the very nature of a prayer burden.

How a Burden Is Communicated

We know that all true prayer burdens are from God, but how does God communicate His burdens to us? Many times He will use something someone says. On other occasions, God may speak to us directly through His Word or in some other way when we are still before Him and listening for Him to speak.

Early one morning a man called me and said, "Charles, I have hesitated to call you because I didn't know how you would respond to what I am about to say. God told me to call and tell you to cancel everything you have planned for the day and spend your time praying."

My first reaction to my friend's call was to go on with business as usual and plan another day for prayer. But God confirmed His instructions in my heart so strongly that I could not resist with a clear conscience.

I called my secretary and told her to cancel everything on my schedule for that day. Then I went to my study and spent the day on my knees. As soon as I started reading my Bible, it was as if every verse said, "Dear Charles." I knew God had something special for me.

It took several weeks for God to show me what He was saying, but I believe that day of fasting and prayer was the spark. It all started because God's burden over my need was communicated to me through a friend's inspired advice.

I believe God could have told me directly, without the intervention of another person—but in this case, He chose to use a friend. The Lord must have known that either I was not listening or my arrangements were so fixed that it would take something unusual to grab my attention. He also knew this would strengthen and deepen the relationship with my friend.

Regardless of how we receive a prayer burden, it is ultimately from God. It may come as a sudden heaviness of heart, or it may come slowly, growing in intensity. Some burdens come both ways. Be careful not to mistake a burden for some physical or emotional problem. Sometimes a burden will drag a person down to where he thinks it is a case of depression. But instead of getting down in the dumps, we are to get down on our knees.

The Weight of a Burden

The next aspect of a prayer burden we must understand is the weight of a burden. In Nehemiah's case, the burden was so great that it caused him to weep and mourn. In fact, he could barely go about his responsibilities. And when he did, his face was so sad that the king noticed.

Not all burdens will take this great of a toll on us, but some *will* cause us to stop everything. When the burden is heavy, Satan is usually quick to tell us to shake it off and keep moving. "You're too busy to worry about that now," he says. But in spite of our pressing responsibilities, we must take the time to get away and spend a few hours (or even days) alone with God in prayer.

All burdens will not require days or even hours of prayer; some burdens may be for something God wants you to do in that moment. For instance, He may burden you to call a friend or give something to the poor. These types of burdens may be understood immediately without a long process of seeking God. But we need to be willing to spend longer times with God when necessary.

Timing Is Important

Once you have decided to take time to seek the Lord, Satan will tempt you to put it off. However, timing is important when following up a burden. When my son was younger, he and some of his friends went whitewater rafting down a river in North Carolina. While on the river, they were involved in rescuing another party of rafters who had lost control of their raft and were being swept toward the most dangerous part of the river. During the rescue, one boy who tried to swim across the river injured his knee and was taken to the hospital.

That evening when the group returned home, a mother of one of the girls asked if everyone was all right. Her voice showed such concern that it was obvious she had been worried. After being questioned about her surprising concern, she explained that during the day the Lord had placed a burden on her heart to pray for the group's safety. As she prayed, the Lord revealed to her that there had been an accident of some kind and that someone had injured a leg.

This wise mother knew the importance of timing in following up a burden. She allowed God to intercede through her during the time of crisis. God used her prayers to keep a bad situation from getting worse.

Worry vs. Burden

At this point, we should distinguish between a worry and a prayer burden. A worry is self-centered, while a burden is God-centered. Worrying focuses our attention on *our* circumstances; God wants our attention focused on *Him*. In fact, He never wants us to focus on the person or thing for which He has burdened us.

The intensity of a burden will be determined by two factors: the *magnitude* of the situation God wants to deal with and the *immediacy* with which God wants to deal with it. When my friend called, he said, "This morning you are to start praying." Immediately I was overwhelmed with a tremendous sense of God's presence and an awesomeness at the burden God was placing on me. God wanted me to do something right at that moment. In Nehemiah's case, the magnitude of the job to be done made his burden heavy. He had a whole city to rebuild with no idea of how to do it.

Sometimes immediacy is important because God sees we are about to run off a cliff. We are headed in a particular direction in life, and everything is going great. Then all of a sudden we sense something isn't right. God burdens our hearts. We feel Him plowing us up and causing us to feel unsure about things.

We examine our lives for sin. Everything checks out, but still something is wrong. This is when we need to stop and ask, "Lord, what are You trying to say?" Only when we stop everything and become quiet do we give God the chance to tell us what He is burdening us about.

He will show us if we are running in the wrong direction. He will reveal to us the direction He would have us go. As we can see, prayer burdens not only get us involved in each other's lives, but they also keep us from making wrong decisions.

The Length of a Burden

Some burdens last longer than others. The length depends on the magnitude of the burden and our response to what God is saying. When we resist a burden, sometimes God will delay His movement in order to get us in a position where we will listen to Him. We should keep in mind that whenever God burdens our hearts about a particular situation, the burden is evidence that He is already working.

This fact should encourage us to pray with perfect faith. A burden is a promise of God's hand in a particular matter. He accomplishes His work primarily through the prayers of His children. By giving us a burden, He gives us an opportunity to build our faith. How? By allowing us to pray for something, He has already started to answer. When God lays a burden on our hearts and we follow up with it faithfully, it is as good as done. There is no need to pray, "If it be Thy will." We *know* it is His will, simply because He has placed the burden on our hearts.

There have been times when God has placed a burden on my heart that lasted for months. At other times burdens have lasted only a few hours. If God requires a drastic change in my life, the burden will stay with me until the change is made. He will keep the pressure on until I focus on Him and seek His guidance.

Nehemiah's burden lasted a long time—so long that it had affected his physical appearance. But while Nehemiah had been praying and seeking God's guidance, God was already working with the king. We don't know in what way, but *something* had been going on. The king not only let Nehemiah and his people go home, but he also gave them all the building materials they needed. Then to top it all off, he sent an armed escort. The king would never have made such a big sacrifice on the spur of the moment just because one of his servants looked a little depressed. God had prepared his heart.

It was only after Nehemiah saw God accomplish all of this that the burden lifted. Nehemiah had been faithful to the burden God had laid on his heart. He was not only faithful in his prayers, but he was also faithful in recognizing the opportunity to be used. He made himself available to be part of the answer to his own prayer.

Sharing Our Burdens

Sharing burdens is a tool God uses to get His work done. But we must be extremely sensitive to God's guidance when we share burdens. Some burdens need to be shared, while others need to be kept private. When we share a burden, it must be done in the spirit of genuine encouragement and love. There must be no criticism.

Many times God will want us to share the burden with only the person we have been burdened for. The timing is very important, because while He is working on us, He is working on them. Once God prepares both parties, then He will allow us to share our burden. Often, when we share a burden, it will be an immediate encouragement to the one for whom we are burdened. People who are hurting need to know they are being prayed for.

Some burdens need to be shared with many people. For instance, if you found out that one of your friends was sick, you would feel burdened to pray. In fact, your concern would not only express itself through your prayers but also through sharing that need with others who could pray. By sharing these types of burdens, God uses us to burden others to pray. God burdened Nehemiah's friends, who in turn shared their burden with Nehemiah. God used this sharing of a burden to lay the same burden on Nehemiah. As a result, the walls of Jerusalem were rebuilt.

I have a personal burden for the United States. I believe this is a burden every American should help shoulder. It grieves my spirit when I see Americans, especially Christians, who don't feel any burden for our nation. This is the type of burden that should be shared by everyone in their own nation.

Personal Blessing

When we follow up a prayer burden and focus on God, we see Him from a new perspective. When this happens, we see ourselves from a new perspective. As a result, all that is hidden in our hearts is revealed. As we pray for someone else, God cleanses us so we can hear what He is saying. When a burden comes, a time of cleansing always follows. Perhaps this is one reason we run from burdens—we don't like to be cleansed. But God knows that the cleaner and more Spirit-filled we are, the more effectively we can pray.

As a result of God cleansing us, we feel a new sense of closeness to Him. We find ourselves loving Him more and serving Him more faithfully. Not only do we love *Him* more but also those around us. With this renewed love for others, we eagerly follow up the burdens God lays on our hearts. A burden, then, is given for the spiritual benefit of everyone involved. When we refuse to take up a burden, we in turn miss a blessing.

Right now your heart may be heavy with a burden from the Lord. You've been trying to shake it off. Maybe you even thought you were ill. The answer is to get on your face before God and tell Him you're willing to receive any burden He has for you. Tell Him you'll stick with it until He accomplishes His purpose.

When you do this, you place yourself in a position to be used by God in someone else's life—either directly or indirectly. But you also allow God to begin cleansing you more deeply than you've ever been cleansed before. You open yourself up to great spiritual blessings.

Are you willing to pray this prayer? *Lord, I am available for any burden You wish to share with me. Don't spare the weight. Use me to the maximum.*

If this is really your heart's desire, you will be amazed when you get to heaven and hear of everything God did through you as a result of your availability to shoulder His burdens.

5

ANSWERED PRAYER

Ask, and it shall be given you; seek, and ye shall find;
knock, and it shall be opened unto you: For every one that
asketh receiveth; and he that seeketh findeth; and to him
that knocketh it shall be opened. Or what man is there of
you, whom if his son ask bread, will he give him a stone?
Or if he ask a fish, will he give him a serpent? If ye then,
being evil, know how to give good gifts unto your children,
how much more shall your Father which is in heaven give
good things to them that ask him? —Matthew 7:7–11

This passage makes prayer appear to be simply a cause-and-effect process. Ask and then receive—as if there is nothing else to it. But often this doesn't happen when we pray. We ask, but we see no results.

We are all interested in answered prayer, but our seemingly unanswered prayers have led many of us not to expect God to respond every time we pray. In fact, when a prayer *is* answered, we are surprised. We know the Bible teaches that God answers prayer. We know He has answered some prayers in our lives. We have seen Him answer the prayers of others. But we still struggle and wonder why He does not seem to answer all the time.

An Encouragement to Pray

First off, Jesus encourages us to pray. He tells us to ask, seek, and knock. We ask for things, we seek understanding, and we knock on doors of opportunity that lie before us. The Lord is saying that in every area of life we can find what we are looking for by talking to the heavenly Father.

Some people question whether we should ask God for material things. The answer is found in Matthew 7:9–10. Wise parents do everything in their power to satisfy their children's needs. This goes for material needs as well as nutritional and spiritual needs. According to verse 11, the material gifts we give our children are proof that God wants to give to us in a similar way but to a greater degree. Do we have a privilege that God has deprived Himself of? No! In fact, there is no way we can outgive God, materially or any other way.

Are We Worth It?

Another hang-up some people have is in regard to their unworthiness to have God answer their prayers. But the basis of all God's answered prayer is His love for us. Calvary settled the question of worth once and for all. According to His love, we are worthy of the greatest gift He had to give—His Son. After that, anything else we ask for is secondary.

Why do we have so much trouble believing God for the minor things in life? It is Satan who says, "Who do you think you are, to ask God for anything?"

To this question there is only one answer: "I am a child of the King. I am so worthy in the eyes of God, He sent His only begotten Son to die for me. If He died for me, certainly He will give me whatever else I need."

There are two opposite schools of thought concerning God's attitude toward blessing us on earth. One group believes we should live in poverty, suffer persecution, and die in poverty as a sacrifice to God. The opposite group believes that all we have to do is ask God and He starts pouring on the blessings; He will give us whatever we ask. According to this group, all we must do is think right. But both of these views are extremes. Neither has the proper balance.

God's Attitude toward Blessing His Children

God loves us and wants to meet all our needs. He wants to give us the desires of our hearts (Ps. 37:4). But God also desires that we seek His face, not just His hand. When our prayers are filled with *I want*, chances are our eyes are on the blessing and not on God. Just as God gives out of love, He desires that we love Him in return. When we love Him, we will seek Him and not just His blessings. To redirect our attention, He will often close the windows of heaven. Otherwise, we would continue on blindly in our error and never seek to know Him the way He intends.

Our heavenly Father loves us so much He wants us to have what we seek. But He will always measure our desires against what He knows is best for us. That's why it is foolish for us to complain when God doesn't answer certain prayers. Since His decisions are in our best interests, we should never try to talk Him into giving us what He has already said we cannot have.

When my family and I first moved to Atlanta, we looked for over a month before we found a suitable house. We had been living with friends up until then. Finally, we found just what we were looking for, and I was thrilled.

I prayed and felt like this was of the Lord, so I applied for a loan. I asked God every day to get that loan approved for us. As a family, we really believed He would; we even thanked Him in advance.

One week later, the bank told me my request for a loan had been turned down. This came as a real shock. To this day, I still don't know the reason they turned me down—and I couldn't understand what God was up to. I asked, "Why didn't He answer our prayers?"

God answered that question the next day by sending a tremendous rainstorm. The basement of the house I almost bought was flooded with a foot of water. My family and I had planned to use the basement for a study and for storage. But God was watching out for us, even when we misunderstood His will. One week later, we found the right house, and enjoyed living there for eight years.

Now that we understand the foundation of God's love for us, we need to understand how to get into a position to allow Him to answer our prayers. The problem is not in God's ability. He can do more than we can ask or think. In fact the problem is not with God at all; the problem is with us.

There are six conditions that must be true in our lives if God is going to answer our prayers.

Right Relationship

First of all, we must have a right relationship with Him. The psalmist wrote, "If I regard iniquity in my heart, the Lord will not hear me" (Ps. 66:18). This does not mean every time we make a mistake God says, "Close up the windows and shut all the doors, no more blessings for that person." If this were true, none of us would ever get anywhere in life.

But if we aim at evil and willfully choose to do evil, the windows of heaven will be shut and God's fellowship broken. This doesn't mean that every time we stumble spiritually God refuses to hear our prayers. He understands where we are and the difficulties we face. But He allows no compromise concerning known sin in our lives.

We must set our sights on God. He must be our aim in life. We must seek to live our lives according to the precepts of His Word and according to the guidance He gives us.

Right Method

The right method answers the question of how we go to the Lord in prayer. The key is to be specific. Jesus says that whatever we believe Him for will become ours in reality. "Therefore I say to you, all things for which you pray and ask, believe that you have received them, and they will be granted you" (Mark 11:24 NASB). In other words, whatever we are able to visualize by faith as ours, God will make it so.

We are not to window-shop when we pray. "Lord, help all the missionaries, and Mom and Dad. Bless the church ..." Praying like that is like walking into a restaurant and telling the waitress we want "food and drink." When we pray vague prayers, it shows that the requests don't really mean much to us. Yet we expect God to get all excited and do something.

Sure, God knows what we are thinking. The problem is that most of the time we don't have anything specific in mind. God could answer prayers like that and we would never know about it. Not only that, He would receive no glory, and we would receive no blessing from seeing a prayer answered.

When the time came for me to buy my daughter a car, I asked her what she wanted. She had been praying and she knew the exact year, model, color, and interior of car she wanted. So we began looking. I had taught her to be specific in her prayers, but I had no idea she would be *that* specific. Regardless of what kind of car we saw or how good the price was, she stuck by what she originally asked God for. This went on for months.

Then one night my son was looking through the want ads and he found a car just like Becky was looking for. It was the right make, color, model, and year. We went to look at it that night, and after talking with the owner for just a few minutes, we knew it was the right car. It didn't take much prayer to know if we were making the right decision; all the praying had been done.

God encourages us to pray specific prayers. Once we decide on something, we must stick with it in our prayers. Otherwise we demonstrate a lack of faith. The psalmist does not say, "He shall give thee the *needs* of thine heart" (see Ps. 37:4). We must understand that what we are asking for is not really the issue. It is the attitude of our hearts that matters. God wants to bless His children, but the relationship and method must be right.

Right Request

The third aspect of prayer we must understand is how to make the right request. "And this is the confidence that we have in him, that, if we ask any thing according to his will, he heareth us" (1 John 5:14). We must ask according to His will. But how do we know if our request is in His will?

First, we must express our desire for what we want from Him. Sometimes we feel guilty for wanting certain things, so we disguise our desires. But if we are to know God's attitude about the thing, we must admit our desires. Then, we must be willing for Him to bring us into complete neutrality—to the point where it really doesn't matter one way or the other. Neutrality means that we want what God wants more than what we want. This may take some time and prayer, but it is an essential step in finding God's will.

Sometimes as soon as we get neutral about something, we lose all our desire for it. This is one way God shows us His will. At other times once we are neutral, God restrains our spirit about the request; we just won't feel peace in asking for it any longer.

Neutrality removes some of the emotion attached to the request. When our emotions are reset on the Lord by becoming neutral, the fog of uncertainty begins to clear. As a result, we can see God's direction more clearly.

Right Formula

When most of us pray, we add "in Jesus' name" to the end of our prayers. For some it is a habit, for others it is considered a magic phrase that assures an answer. We read John 14:14 and mistakenly decide that the only qualification to having our prayers answered is to say "in Jesus' name." This is an error because of another qualification: We must abide (John 15:7).

Praying in Jesus' name is more than a phrase we add to a prayer; it is the character of the prayer itself. To pray in Jesus' name means that we are asking something because it is in character with what Jesus would ask if He were in our circumstances. It means that the prayer is in keeping with His nature and character as He lives His life through us. Since He indwells us, He not only desires to live through us but to intercede through us as well.

Many times we make what appear to be mundane requests. But they are real needs to us, and God is willing to meet them. Whether they are for spiritual or material needs, it makes little difference to Him; He is our loving Father who delights in meeting all of our needs. But before we add "in Jesus' name" on the end, we must make sure everything in the prayer is in keeping with His character.

Right Attitudes

The book of James describes the attitude we are to have when making requests. When we come to God and doubt if we are in His will in making a request, we are wavering Christians. We often feel confident about making a request then talk with friends only to have them tell us we are wrong. Back and forth we are tossed; should we, or shouldn't we? James wrote about the wavering Christian: "Let not that man think that he shall receive any thing of the Lord" (James 1:7).

Doubt and prayer do not mix. Doubt comes from relying on feelings and others' opinions. A man whose faith wavers in prayer is a "double minded man" and is "unstable in all his ways" (v. 8). He is not just unstable in his prayer life but in all his ways. Our faith in God determines our course in life—for if our faith in Him wavers, where else will we put our security?

In the winter of 1981, our church was offered the opportunity to purchase a block and a half of property adjacent to our facilities. The cost was $2,850,000 in cash at closing. The bank was willing to lend us the money at 21 percent interest. But I didn't believe that God wanted us to borrow the money. He wanted to build our faith.

In the previous twelve months, our congregation had given over $1,200,000 for additional property and renovations. Two weeks before the deadline, we had only $125,000 more. It looked impossible—especially in light of how much the people had already given.

On Sunday morning I preached from 1 Chronicles 29, which is the account of Israel's response to David's challenge to provide funds to build the temple. At the close of the first morning service, a young man offered his wedding band for the fund. It was the only possession of any value he and his wife had. They had been robbed the week before and had lost everything else.

At the second service, I preached the same sermon and shared the sacrificial spirit of the couple. At the close of the message, I invited people to be saved or to unite with our fellowship. People lined up across the front of the sanctuary and up and down the aisles. They gave diamond rings, bracelets, pendants, watches, necklaces; they promised cars, campers, stocks and bonds, and so forth. By the following Friday we had $1,350,000.

When I thought about how much money was given and how much more we needed, my faith nose-dived. But when I spent time alone with God in prayer, it was always the same message: "Trust Me."

I soon saw a pattern. When I would try to figure out just how we could come up with the money, my faith would waver. But as long as I accepted my utter helplessness, my faith soared like an eagle.

When I stepped into the pulpit on the following Sunday (with the deadline twenty-four hours away), we still needed an additional $1,500,000. As I looked out across the sea of faces, it all seemed so impossible. But I knew what I had to do. God and I had settled that the day before.

I had spent the previous Saturday in prayer, wrestling with my weak and wavering faith. God spoke to me very clearly. I must publicly declare that we would not borrow any money; we must trust the

Lord to provide our needs and to prove Himself faithful. He pointed me to Isaiah 50:7–11 for a word of encouragement and warning.

As I shared this challenge with the people, I made it clear that we wouldn't borrow any money. "We must burn every bridge and cut off every avenue of escape. Our faith must be in Him and Him alone," I said.

I held up a strand of hair and cut it with scissors as a symbol of cutting off all routes of retreat. When I did that, something happened to the congregation. They were released. By that Sunday evening they gave an additional $1 million. Thirty minutes before the deadline, we had our $2,850,000.

What then is the right attitude? Jesus summed it up. "What things soever ye desire, when ye pray, believe that ye receive them, and ye shall have them" (Mark 11:24). Faith is the capacity to visualize what is not as if it had already happened. Once we visualize it, we must act on what we know to be true by faith. Our faith must not be based on how we feel or what our five senses tell us but on what God says in His Word. Feelings and circumstances change, but God never changes. The right attitude is one of faith.

Right Motive

Finally, we must have right motives. Christ said, "Let your light so shine before men, that they may see your good works, and glorify your Father which is in heaven" (Matt. 5:16). Our motives for everything we do must be to glorify the Father.

Can a prayer for some mundane, seemingly unimportant material thing give glory to God? Yes! But only if we are willing to share the need or desire being met as a testimony to others of God's faithfulness. In this way, God will receive glory out of any prayer He answers.

When people hear of a specific request being answered, their faith is strengthened. In this way, God will receive glory out of any prayer He answers.

What we ask for is really insignificant compared with the glory God will receive. When we set our sights in prayer on giving God glory rather than just getting what we're asking for, God will delight in answering our prayers.

If we want our prayers to affect God, we must: (1) begin with a right relationship with Him through Jesus Christ; (2) make specific requests; (3) pray according to His will for us; (4) pray in Jesus' name and in keeping with His character; (5) ask in faith that is based on God's Word, not on feelings or on others' opinions; and (6) pray with the right motives. All we do, say, and pray must be to the glory of God.

If your prayers aren't being answered, check out these six conditions. It is God's desire and joy to answer your prayers. I pray that you will put yourself in a position that will allow Him to do just that.

6

WHY OUR PRAYERS ARE UNANSWERED

But without faith it is impossible to please him: for he that cometh to God must believe that he is, and that he is a rewarder of them that diligently seek him. —*Hebrews 11:6*

A member of our church came into my office one afternoon weeping over her husband's decision to divorce her. She could not understand what had prompted his decision, but she was willing to do whatever she could to rebuild their marriage. After we talked, we both decided to commit ourselves to pray.

Frances was fervent in her prayers. She fasted and prayed with such urgency that many of her friends joined her prayer campaign. Soon, everyone involved believed that her husband would change his mind and that God would rebuild Frances's home.

Six months later, however, the divorce was finalized. Frances and her fourteen-year-old son were left with almost nothing. But she persevered in prayer, sure that God would soften her husband's heart. Once again, people all over the church joined Frances in prayer.

Then one morning Frances's husband called and told her about his plans to marry a younger woman. This devastated Frances. When she came into my office later that day, she looked at me through swollen eyes and asked, "Dr. Stanley, why didn't God answer my prayer?"

Frances's question is one that has crossed the mind of every child of God who has prayed seemingly fruitless prayers. Many people ignore seemingly unanswered prayer. But in a case such as Frances's, the hurt was too big to ignore. Why *didn't* God answer her prayer?

There are things we will never know in this lifetime. But as to the issue of answered prayer, God has not left us to wonder. Prayer is not meant to be a game of hit or miss. We aren't slaves left to catch crumbs from the Master's table when He chooses to throw them our way (Matt. 15:27).

Prayer is a child making a request of the Father. And just like any good earthly father, our heavenly Father is willing to tell us why we cannot have certain things. But before He will tell us, we must ask (James 4:2).

God *does* answer all prayers; He answers *yes, no,* or *wait.* Let's look at those instances when God says no. All of us have asked God for things at one time or another and not received what we asked for. We can make as many excuses as we want, but the truth is that God didn't do what we asked Him to do.

Usually when a prayer is answered no, we look for sin in our lives. Sometimes this *is* the problem, but many times there is nothing to confess. Yet our prayers still are answered no. Let's address this question first: Why does God answer no, when to the best of our knowledge we are absolutely clean before Him?

We Must Seek God

God wants us to seek Him more than anything else, even more than we seek answers to prayer. When we come to God in prayer, sometimes our hearts are so full of what we want that we leave God out. Our minds become consumed with the gift rather than the Giver.

This is the basic problem with most prayers. Every other reason we discuss concerning unanswered prayer in some way or another relates back to this. If we are not careful, God becomes a means to an end. But God desires to be the end; it is His desire that we seek Him and Him alone.

God has predestined us, according to His will, to be conformed to the image of His Son (Rom. 8:29). In God's eyes, the most important thing is that we experience Christ's life in us. This does not necessarily mean He is going to give us everything we ask for. On the contrary, He will allow us to have only those things that are in keeping with His ultimate will.

Unfortunately for us, we forget the big picture in our prayers. We focus on our immediate needs and desires and forget what God is ultimately trying to do: conform us to His image (Col. 3:10). Even when our sins are confessed and nothing is standing in the way of our relationship with the Father, He will withhold answers to prayer if He sees we need to refocus our attention on Him.

We Must Trust Him

God also withholds answers to teach us to trust Him. If God gave us everything we wanted every time we asked Him for something, what would happen? Before long, we would take Him for granted. As a result, we would miss out on one of God's greatest blessings: learning to trust Him.

Receiving something the minute we ask for it requires no faith. Yet without faith it is impossible to please Him (Heb. 11:6). God wants to know if we still believe He will keep His word when we have no tangible evidence to hold on to. We are usually tossed to and fro between what God's Word says and what we see and hear. But God uses this struggle to build our faith (James 1:2–3). To quit asking and believing is to call God a liar. To quit praying and believing is to give more credit to our understanding of a situation than to God's omnipotent wisdom.

God does not withhold His answers to taunt us or to toy with our emotions. By withholding His answers, He teaches us to persist in prayer, to keep our eyes focused on Him, and to ignore our feelings. He desires for us to believe Him strictly on the basis of what He says in His Word, regardless of what we see. As we allow God to prove Himself faithful in situation after situation, it becomes easier to trust Him.

He Is Preparing Us

Another reason God withholds answers is because He is in the process of preparing us. Many young people pray and pray that the Lord will send a marriage partner. As they get into their late twenties or thirties, many question God's interest in their situations. They say, "What is God waiting for?" He may be waiting until He knows they are ready.

As I grow older and look back on life, it is clear that if God had answered certain prayers according to my timing, I would have missed His best in every case. Much of what we pray for is in the will of God, but our timing is off.

Let us say, for instance, your five-year-old son wants a pocketknife and a flashlight. You might not mind giving him the flashlight, but he needs to grow up a little before you can trust him with the knife. In the same way, God is waiting for us to grow spiritually in some areas before He can allow us to experience all the spiritual and material blessings He has in store (Eph. 1:3).

Sometimes God Has Something Better

A fourth reason God withholds answers to our prayers is because He wants to give us something better than we asked for. It may be more than we deserve, more than we ask for, and more than we expect.

One beautiful example of this is the story of Lazarus (John 11). If Jesus had healed Lazarus immediately, we would have missed one of Jesus' greatest miracles. But Jesus seemingly ignored Mary and Martha's pleas to save their brother. Just like us, they didn't understand why Jesus waited. But which is the greater blessing—having a man healed or having him raised from the dead? What at first was interpreted as insensitivity turned out to be a glorious experience for everyone involved.

In 1971, our church's television broadcast was taken off the air because of conflict within the church. After the conflict was resolved, we asked the same network if they would reschedule us at the same broadcast time they had given us before. But they refused to sell us the time.

We believed God wanted us on television, but for some reason things were not working out. So we prayed that God would once again allow us to begin a television ministry. When we started praying, we thought something would open up soon. But a year passed before anything happened.

Eventually we were invited by two different stations to participate in their weekly programming. Instead of being broadcasted in black and white like before, our program was in color. One opportunity led to another, and today our service is broadcast around the world.

God didn't answer our prayer to be put right back on the air for a reason. He waited and provided us with something much better than we asked for.

These are four reasons God withholds a blessing or answer to prayer when the condition of our hearts is not the deciding factor. God's perspective encompasses more than ours; He has His overall purpose for our lives in mind.

It would be great to say that these are the only four reasons God doesn't answer prayer, but there are more. The next seven reasons involve areas we must deal with before God will answer our prayers, and in some cases, before He will even hear our prayers.

Family Relationships

First, prayers are hindered when our home relationships are not right (1 Peter 3:1–7). Think about it: How can we have fellowship with a loving, heavenly Father who is forgiving and gracious and at the same time treat our family members with no consideration? If we allow resentment, bitterness, and indifference to build up between members of our families, then our prayers will be hindered. The word *hindered* in verse 7 means to put an obstacle in the way of something. Our conflicts at home may be insurmountable obstacles to our prayers.

I have heard story after story of people who received answers to prayer after they made things right at home. A close friend of mine was constantly struggling to keep his head above water in his business. We had prayed together many times for God to restore his failing business. But regardless of how much or how earnestly we prayed, things didn't change.

Then one day he shared how the Lord had convicted him about some areas in his marriage that he had refused to deal with. These were problems he knew existed but had done nothing about. When he dealt with these problems, God renewed his relationship with his wife. In addition, his business turned completely around. Soon things were better financially than ever before. But more importantly his home, which had been a place of constant conflict, became a place of peace.

Unresolved horizontal conflicts make for unresolved vertical conflicts. As long as things aren't right in our families, things won't be right between us and God. If He answers our prayers while we are out of fellowship with other people, He would in a sense be condoning our disobedience. But God will never condone or overlook sin; He hates sin. Our disobedience directly opposes what He ultimately wants to accomplish in our lives. Therefore, it must be dealt with. So what does the Father do? He closes the door of heaven and locks it up until we straighten out our family relationships.

Someone might say, "I have had unresolved conflicts with my family for a long time, and God has answered *my* prayers." This may appear to be true, but according to Scripture, God will not hear that person's prayers. We forget that other people are praying too, and God may be showing mercy to other members of our families while He waits for us to get straightened out. Regardless of what we think is happening, God won't answer our own prayers if we have unresolved family conflicts.

I believe the church is so weak because there is so much prayerlessness. People are still talking to God, but God is not listening. When there are difficulties and heartaches at home, we must confess to each other right then and there; we must ask for forgiveness when it is necessary. If we regard iniquity in our hearts—bitterness, wrong attitudes, or an ungrateful spirit—heaven will be closed to our prayers.

Jesus said, "For if ye forgive men their trespasses, your heavenly Father will also forgive you: But if ye forgive not men their trespasses, neither will your Father forgive your trespasses" (Matt. 6:14–15). If we have an unforgiving spirit toward someone, that in itself is a sin. Therefore, if we confess our sins and yet refuse to forgive our brother or sister, then we have not repented of having an unforgiving spirit. This will be a hindrance to our prayers.

For years people will cling to unconfessed bitterness and hatred toward a family member. They become angry with God for not answering their prayers, while all along *they* are the problem—not God. Many people like this eventually become bitter against the church and turn their backs on Christianity altogether. The problem is in our perspective. We don't see unsettled family quarrels and misunderstandings as sin—but God does.

Why would God allow such seemingly small things to hinder our prayers? Even the smallest sin is a stumbling block to what God has in store for us. We cannot entertain bitterness, resentment, and criticism and expect God to answer our prayers—He won't do it. He is not the slightest bit interested in our prayers when we harbor sin in our lives, except for our prayers of repentance. We must make things right horizontally before we can have much impact vertically.

We Must Check Our Motives

Another reason God does not answer our prayers is because of our wrong motives, which, as we learned in the last chapter, are important to evaluate before approaching the Lord. "Ye ask, and receive not, because ye ask amiss, that ye may consume it upon your lusts" (James 4:3). In other words, we are often more interested in our desires than we are in glorifying God. Christ said that His work was to glorify the Father (John 17:4). This must be our work as well. We must learn to pray in a fashion that brings more glory to God than to ourselves. We must pray with a spirit of gratitude, thanksgiving, and praise. We must show our appreciation for the many blessings He has so faithfully given us. He has blessed us, not because we deserve it, but because He loves us. At the same time we must commit ourselves to be good stewards of whatever He gives us, including the opportunities that come our way.

It all goes back to God's perspective—we must see the big picture. Any other perspective will center our prayers ultimately on us.

One way to keep a check on your motivation is to stop after a few minutes of prayer and ask yourself, *How did I start this prayer? Did I just jump in and start asking? Or did I start off praising the Lord and showing my gratitude for what He has already done for me?* We must be honest with ourselves and check our motives in regard to every request we make.

We Must Have Unwavering Faith

We have already discussed the fact that God sometimes waits in order to teach us to trust Him. But many times God cannot answer us because of our lack of faith. All of us have some measure of faith, but many times we go to God with wavering faith. James said in relation to prayer, "But let him ask in faith, nothing wavering. For he that wavereth is like a wave of the sea driven with the wind and tossed. For let not that man think that he shall receive any thing of the Lord" (James 1:6–7).

We may have some initial apprehension about certain requests. But as God confirms His approval through His Word, the wavering should cease. God uses this initial wavering to test and stretch our faith. But He never intended this to be the normal state of prayer. Wavering faith is not the faith God responds to.

Focus on His Word

We are not to look at what is happening—we are to look in His Word. The Bible is the anchor of our faith. Regardless of what kinds of storms come our way, regardless of our circumstances, we are to keep looking at the Word. He wants our prayers to be God-centered, Christ-centered, and Spirit-centered—not thing-centered, trial-centered, and circumstance-centered. For if our prayers are centered on anything other than the Lord, our faith will waver. Why? Because He is the only firm, unchanging foundation on which to base anything—especially our prayers.

All of us have some measure of faith. We often look at others and envy their faith, thinking that our prayers would be more readily answered if we had their faith. This may be true, but we must keep in mind that God is in the process of building our faith. Each prayer is an opportunity to grow. We must learn to pray for things with our eyes and hearts full of God. We must learn then to wait, disregarding what we see and feel, until God leads us otherwise.

Selfishness Hinders Our Prayers

The next reason God does not answer our prayers is because we are stingy. "Whoso stoppeth his ears at the cry of the poor, he also shall cry himself, but shall not be heard" (Prov. 21:13). If we refuse to listen to someone in need, can we expect God to listen to our prayers and meet our needs? That would be an absolute contradiction of Christ's entire message. We cannot turn a deaf ear to someone who is in need because we don't have time or don't want to be bothered and then expect God to bless us. He doesn't work that way.

For example, can a person who refuses to tithe and give to the poor or to missionaries expect God to bless him financially? This is hypocrisy. To bless a man such as this would be to encourage him to live in total opposition to what God intends. Besides, anyone who claims to be a Christian and claims that God is meeting all of his needs yet does not tithe is a liar.

God uses both our needs and His blessings to teach us to trust Him. But when we become stingy with God's blessings, they stop. When we turn a deaf ear to known needs, our prayers will in no way prompt God to any action on our behalf. We have freely received; we must freely give.

Indifference to God's Word

God will not answer our prayers if we are indifferent to His Word. "He that turneth away his ear from hearing the law, even his prayer shall be [an] abomination" (Prov. 28:9). He intends for our souls to be "crushed" with a desire for His Word, as the psalmist teaches (Ps. 119:20 NASB). We should be constantly seeking the deeper truths of Scripture. God sent the Holy Spirit into each of us so that we might understand for ourselves what the Father has to say through His Word.

Many Christians have turned their backs on the Bible, either out of lack of understanding or lack of conviction. Others don't mind hearing God's Word, but they make no attempt to understand it or apply it to their lives.

God detests the prayers of a man who has no delight in His Word. When we live with a closed Bible, we live with a closed heaven; God will not answer our prayers.

Unconfessed Sin

The final reason God doesn't answer prayer is unconfessed sin. It must be clear that unconfessed sin short-circuits prayer. Isaiah wrote, "Behold, the LORD's hand is not shortened, that it cannot save; neither his ear heavy, that it cannot hear: But your iniquities have separated between you and your God, and your sins have hid his face from you, that he will not hear" (Isa. 59:1–2). It is not that God *cannot* hear; but He *will* not hear. Our unconfessed sin causes God to turn His back on our prayers, refusing to listen. He will not put a spiritual crowbar into our lives and open us up; He will just wait.

We can pray and pray, but the Father will not move an inch until we confess our sins. He wants us voluntarily to open our hearts and allow Him to cleanse us. If we are going to pray, we shouldn't waste our time when God isn't listening. And besides, what sin is worth more to us than a relationship with God? Nothing is more valuable than unhindered, two-way communication with Him. In fact, He desires this for us more than we desire it for ourselves.

Now is the time to take each unanswered prayer to the Lord and ask Him why He is not responding. He may point out some sin in your life, or He may refocus your attention on His face. Whatever the situation, don't continue to make excuses for God in regard to your unanswered prayers. In every situation He is seeking to conform you to the image of His Son. As you keep this in mind, you'll pray more in line with God's will—and you'll see more answered prayers as a result.

7

HOW TO PRAY IN THE WILL OF GOD

And this is the confidence that we have in him,

that, if we ask any thing according to his will,

he heareth us: And if we know that he hears us,

whatsoever we ask, we know that we have the petitions

that we desired of him. —*1 John 5:14–15*

How can I know that my prayer request is in keeping with the will of God? How will I know that my petition is pleasing to the Father? Can I be sure that what I am asking is right?

These are among the most legitimate and frequently asked questions about prayer. What is more discouraging than praying when you aren't sure your request is compatible with God's plan?

On the other hand, what greater motivation for prayer can we have than to approach the Father with unwavering confidence that our request has His divine approval?

Some prayer requests need not be sifted through the will of God, for the Bible is unmistakably clear about some things. We never have to pray: "Lord, save my dad from his life of sin *if it be Thy will.*" Jesus said, "I am come to seek and to save that which is lost" (see Luke 19:10). God "is longsuffering to us-ward, not willing that any should perish, but that all should come to repentance" (2 Peter 3:9).

Whenever the Bible is specific and clear in its promises, we can pray with confidence. No one ever need pray, "Lord, help me to be forgiving toward those who have wronged me, *if it be Thy will.*" Our Lord makes it very clear as to what our attitude should be toward those who wrong us. "And be ye kind one to another, tenderhearted, forgiving one another, even as God for Christ's sake hath forgiven you" (Eph. 4:32).

We do not always have such specific direction about our petitions. Yet He will guide us in our prayers to pray in accordance with His will.

When Jesus said, "Ask, and it shall be given you; seek, and ye shall find; knock, and it shall be opened unto you" (Matt. 7:7), He indicated His desire to meet our needs. Paul wrote that we are to "be careful for nothing; but in every thing by prayer and supplication with thanksgiving let your requests be made known unto God" (Phil. 4:6). The passage in 1 John 5:14–15 at the beginning of this chapter shows us the same truth—God wants us to ask Him to take care of our needs.

At first it seems quite simple. All we have to do is ask, and God gets busy answering our prayers. But there is really more to it than that. God puts conditions on His promises. These conditions are for our own good; they aren't excuses for God not to answer our prayers. "This is the confidence that we have in him, that, if we ask any thing according to his will, he heareth us" (1 John 5:14). This is the condition—that we ask according to His will. But how do we know if we are praying in God's will?

Shooting in the Dark

At times all of us feel that our prayers are shooting in the dark. We feel as though a particular request is right at the moment, but when we don't see an immediate answer, we wonder if it was ever God's will to begin with. Our faith decreases instead of increases because we never have any real assurance of what we are praying for. So we shoot in the dark and hope that God will be in agreement and will respond favorably.

This is not the way God wants His people praying. What good does it do to pray if we don't have any hint of what to pray for? That would be a waste of His time and ours. But His Word gives us clear direction on how to find His will in prayer.

A Threefold Promise

God makes us a threefold promise in 1 John 5:14–15. First, He promises to listen if we pray according to His will. Second, He promises that we already possess what we have asked for. Third, He promises that *we know* that we have the petitions we desire. So when we pray according to His will, He hears us, we have what we ask for, and *we know* that we have what we ask for.

The word *confidence* in verse 14 means boldness or assurance. Among the Greeks, this word was used as a political term and referred to the freedom to speak publicly. So as children of God, we can go to Him openly and boldly to make our requests. Even the mood of the verb *ask* indicates the idea of making a personal request.

We must forget the notion that we cannot ask anything for ourselves. That is not what Scripture teaches. These two verses deal with our capacity to approach God openly, freely, confidently, and boldly with the assurance that He will hear and grant what we ask. As a result, we know that we will have what we ask for.

But now back to this matter of praying in God's will. We say, "Oh, *that's* the catch." And in one sense, it *is* a catch. For many sincere, well-meant prayers have gone unanswered as a result of our praying out of God's will. Can we always know the will of God in our prayers? Yes, although not always at first. Sometimes when we go to God, we are in the dark—we don't know what to ask for. So in the beginning we do not know His will. But if we can understand and apply certain principles, ultimately we can know God's will as we pray.

Stumbling Blocks

Satan throws three stumbling blocks in our way to keep us from finding God's will when we pray. He says, "How can you make a request in faith when you don't know if God is in agreement with you? And if you aren't sure that God agrees with your prayers, why waste your time praying in the first place?"

But if we decide to pray anyway, Satan taunts us. "Look at your past," he says. "You don't have the right to ask God for anything. God isn't going to listen to *you*." At this point, we get our self-esteem mixed up with whether our request is of God. So we either quit praying, or pray and tack on to the end "if it be Your will."

If we end all our prayers with "if it be Your will," what do we have? Uncertainty! We don't have any assurance of any answer. This brings us to the passage in the book of James that says, "Whereas ye know not what shall be on the morrow. For what is your life? It is even a vapour, that appeareth for a little time, and then vanisheth away. For that ye ought to say, If the Lord will, we shall live, and do this, or that" (James 4:14–15). This passage is not referring to prayer but to presumption in planning for the future.

For some people, Matthew 26:39 is the reason their prayers end with that little phrase. There, Jesus was praying in the garden of Gethsemane. Some say, "Jesus didn't know for sure if He had to die on the cross, so He just left it up to the Father to make the decision." But that isn't what happened. The cup did not symbolize the cross. Jesus knew that He had to die. In Matthew 16:21, He even spoke of His death. So what was the cup He referred to?

Though our minds cannot comprehend it, there has never been a time when Jesus was not alive. When He came to earth, He was God—the same God who has always been, even before the creation of the universe. On earth, Jesus became a man, but He was still God in every way. When He went to the garden, He wasn't afraid to die; the cup of which He spoke was not death but something far worse for Him. He knew that He would have to bear the sins of the whole world on Himself. He was struggling with the coming separation from His Father.

Scripture shows that Jesus wasn't questioning whether to obey His Father. The issue was whether there was any other way to atone for man's sin besides His separation from the Father. It is impossible for us to conceive of the closeness Jesus has with the Father. In the same way it is impossible for us to understand what He felt in those moments when He knew that He would be banished from the Father's presence. But even in that intense struggle, Christ was committed to obedience: "Not as I will, but as thou wilt" (Matt. 26:39). Even in those struggling hours He knew exactly what God's will was. God never left His Son to doubt, and in the same way He will never let us doubt when we are sincerely seeking His will.

Sometimes when we aren't sure about God's will, we put out a fleece. In a sense, we make a deal with God. We say, "If this happens, then I will do 'A.' But if that happens, then I will do 'B.'" Seeking God's will in this way is a sign of immaturity. This kind of reasoning leaves no room for any real faith and was never intended to be the normal way to discover God's will. So what approach should we take when we aren't sure how to pray?

Paul prayed for the believers in Colossae to "be filled with the knowledge of his will in all wisdom and spiritual understanding" (Col. 1:9). James wrote, "If any of you lack wisdom, let him ask of God, that giveth to all men liberally, and upbraideth not; and it shall be given him" (James 1:5). What is wisdom? It is seeing things from God's perspective. When we do not know what God thinks about our requests, we have a right to ask Him.

Paul wrote, "Likewise the Spirit also helpeth our infirmities: for we know not what we should pray for as we ought: but the Spirit [Himself] maketh intercession for us with groanings which cannot be uttered" (Rom. 8:26). The word *infirmities* does not mean illnesses; it refers to spiritual weaknesses—our inability to pray from God's perspective. In other words, the Spirit will pray through us when we don't understand what to pray, and at the same time He will give us understanding. So when we pray without understanding, we aren't wasting our time, as Satan would have us believe. On the contrary, God is honoring our prayers.

As we continue to pray, God will reveal His will to us. Jesus promised, "Howbeit when he, the Spirit of truth, is come, he will guide you into all truth" (John 16:13). Part of the Holy Spirit's task is to guide us into the truth of how we should pray. But He will only do this if we are praying. It is essential that we have a desire to pray in accordance with His will; this is the attitude God honors.

How to Begin

So assuming there is no sin in our lives and we really want to know God's will when we pray, how should we start? First, we must decide if we are asking Him to give us something we want, something we need, or some direction in a matter. Second, we should ask God to give us a passage of Scripture that relates in some way to our request—a passage we can meditate on and through which God can speak to us.

Most Christians overlook the importance of Scripture in prayer. But the more we saturate our minds with the Word of God, the more we will become familiar with God's way. Then it will be easier for us to distinguish His will from our own thoughts. The Father desires that we know Him more than He desires to answer our prayers. He wants to use each prayer as a tool to familiarize us with His ways, His thoughts, and His desires. If we omit His Word in our prayer lives, we miss the ultimate blessing of prayer—knowing God.

Ask the Lord to give you a particular promise from Scripture dealing with your request. Make this the anchor of your faith in this area. Hold on to that verse, regardless of what happens or how you feel. Live by it, pray by it, and refuse to give in until you have whatever it is God has promised.

Since God wants us to know His will in our prayers, and since we know that if we are praying according to His will we already have the things we ask for, the next step is to begin thanking Him. There is no need to keep asking Him to do what we have already asked Him to do. In the same way, there is no need to beg Him to do what He has already promised to do. Instead, we should thank Him for it. We should thank Him for the wisdom we are going to experience in our prayers. We should thank Him for granting our desires, meeting our needs, and giving us direction.

Then we must wait. More asking will show a lack of faith. It is at this point, however, that our faith will be tested the most. We may want to add "if it is Your will" to our prayers, just in case we misunderstood. This is why basing our prayers on Scripture is so important—it gives us a foundation. God's Word is unchanging truth. It is in the protected harbor of His Word that we bring our faith to rest.

When we go to God, instead of asking, "Lord, please do this and that," let's ask Him to show us how to pray. Let's ask the Holy Spirit to pray through us from beginning to end. Then we can be assured of praying according to His will. We will pray for things we would never think to pray for otherwise. As we pray, God will show us a side of prayer we have never seen.

When our hearts are clean and we have committed ourselves to obey Him yet we have no clue as to what to pray, God takes the responsibility of showing us. He may use Scripture, or He may use circumstances. If our request isn't in keeping with His will, He will redirect our attention to Him, and we will lose interest in what we are asking. Regardless of how He shows us, we must believe that He will. Often we will have to wait. But it is during these times of waiting that we begin to really know God.

As we find God's will in our prayers, He confirms it by filling our hearts with the peace of the Holy Spirit. "Be careful for nothing; but in every thing by prayer and supplication with thanksgiving let your requests be made known unto God. And the peace of God, which passeth all understanding, shall keep your hearts and minds through Christ Jesus" (Phil. 4:6–7). We can know without doubt that we are on His track in our prayers. When this is true, we can pray with the assurance that Christ is praying with us to the same end. Peace in our hearts is God's seal of approval on our prayers.

God desires to give us direction in our prayers. He has promised in His Word to do so. Our responsibility is to seek His direction through Scripture. Once we have found His promise to us, we must dig in and wait while thanking Him for what is already ours. For "if God be for us" (Rom. 8:31) in our prayers, who or what can stand against us?

8
A TIME TO WAIT, A TIME TO ACT

*But the children of Israel committed a trespass in the accursed
thing: for Achan, the son of Carmi, the son of Zabdi, the son
of Zerah, of the tribe of Judah, took of the accursed thing:
and the anger of the LORD was kindled against the children
of Israel. And Joshua sent men from Jericho to Ai, which is
beside Bethaven, on the east of Bethel, and spake unto them,
saying, Go up and view the country. And the men went up
and viewed Ai. And they returned to Joshua, and said unto
him, Let not all the people go up; but let about two or three
thousand men go up and smite Ai; and make not all the
people to labour thither; for they are but few. So there went
up thither of the people about three thousand men: and they
fled before the men of Ai. And the men of Ai smote of them
about thirty and six men: for they chased them from before
the gate even unto Shebarim, and smote them in the going
down: wherefore the hearts of the people melted, and became as*

water. And Joshua rent his clothes, and fell to the earth upon
his face before the ark of the LORD until the eventide, he and
the elders of Israel, and put dust upon their heads. And Joshua
said, Alas, O LORD God, wherefore hast thou at all brought
this people over Jordan, to deliver us into the hand of the
Amorites, to destroy us? Would to God we had been content,
and dwelt on the other side [of] Jordan! O LORD, what shall
I say, when Israel turneth their backs before their enemies!
For the Canaanites and all the inhabitants of the land shall
hear of it, and shall environ us round, and cut off our name
from the earth: and what wilt thou do unto thy great name?

And the LORD said unto Joshua, Get thee up; wherefore liest
thou thus upon thy face? Israel hath sinned, and they have
also transgressed my covenant which I commanded them: for
they have even taken of the accursed thing, and have also
stolen, and dissembled also, and they have put it even among
their own stuff. Therefore the children of Israel could not
stand before their enemies, but turned their backs before their
enemies, because they were accursed: neither will I be with
you any more, except ye destroy the accursed from among
you. Up, sanctify the people, and say, Sanctify yourselves
against to morrow: for thus saith the LORD God of Israel,
There is an accursed thing in the midst of thee, O Israel:
thou canst not stand before thine enemies, until ye take away
the accursed thing from among you. —Joshua 7:1–13

Imagine for a moment that you lost your job. You know God allowed it to happen for a reason, but you aren't sure what that reason is. You know He wants to teach you something, but what is the next step? Should you just sit and do nothing, waiting for God to act? Or should you go out and look for another job?

Sometimes God wants us to wait. But sometimes when a situation arises, God challenges us to do something. This particular passage in Joshua is an example.

Background

The people of Israel crossed the Jordan River and faced the fortified city of Jericho (Josh. 6). God told Joshua two things. First of all, He promised him that Jericho would fall to the nation of Israel. Then, God revealed the military strategy that Joshua was to use. Humanly speaking, this appeared to be the most naïve, ridiculous strategy any commander could pursue. Whoever heard of conquering an enemy by marching around their city once a day for six days, and then on the seventh day marching around it seven times, blowing trumpets, and shouting? But it worked. God was in it.

When God gives directions, they are precise and detailed. He doesn't give us commands and then leave us to figure them out alone. He gave Joshua explicit instructions as to how Jericho should be taken. He told him when to march, how many times the soldiers were to circle the city, when to shout, and when to be quiet. God knew that if He allowed them to talk, they would have probably murmured against Joshua for his unorthodox strategy. So God specifically told Joshua to keep them quiet.

As a result of their obedience, the nation of Israel experienced tremendous victory. Everyone was praising the Lord and shouting "glory" for what God had done. So Joshua, on the basis of that overwhelming victory, sent spies into the next city to be taken. The spies returned, confident that Ai would be a pushover. They told Joshua that only a couple thousand men would be needed to take the city. And why not? After all, look what they had accomplished at Jericho. The truth was *they* didn't do anything at Jericho; *God* did it all.

Because of their previous victory, the Israelites became over-confident and proud. They no longer felt the need to wait for God's directions. Overconfidence is a satanic trap, and they fell for it.

Calamity struck at Ai because Joshua didn't listen for God's promise and God's strategy; he listened instead to his own cohorts. The soldiers of Ai came rushing out of the city and routed the Israelites, killing thirty-six men. The Israelites returned home discouraged and disillusioned. "The hearts of the people melted, and became as water" (Josh. 7:5). They were so overwhelmed with fright that they lost all heart for battle.

Joshua's Prayer

So we find Joshua crying out before God. "Joshua rent his clothes, and fell to the earth upon his face before the ark of the LORD until the eventide, he and the elders of Israel, and put dust upon their heads" (Josh. 7:6). Tearing his clothes was an outward sign of his grief. Falling on his face before the ark was a sign of his humbling himself before the Lord.

So Joshua prayed:

> Alas, O LORD God, wherefore last thou
> at all brought this people over Jordan, to
> deliver us into the hands of the Amorites,
> to destroy us? Would to God we had been
> content, and dwelt on the other side [of]
> Jordan! O LORD, what shall I say, when
> Israel turneth their backs before their
> enemies! For the Canaanites and all the
> inhabitants of the land shall hear of it,
> and shall environ us round, and cut off
> our name from the earth: and what wilt
> thou do unto thy great name? (vv. 7–9)

Joshua's prayer sounded much like the prayers of the Israelites as they wandered in the wilderness. It seems they would have learned to trust God after that experience. But Joshua was repeating the same old lines, "Oh, God, why did You allow us to get into this mess? Why didn't You leave us over on the other side of Canaan?"

Joshua didn't mention a single promise from God in his prayer; there was no thanksgiving for the good things God had done and no praise for the Lord either. In fact, his prayer was one of total defeat; this shows what he had his eyes on.

We have all come to God at times with this kind of prayer. We cry out, "Oh, Lord, why did You let me get into such a mess? Why do You treat me this way?" We blame God for our unpleasant circumstances. But look at what God told Joshua: "Get thee up; wherefore liest thou thus upon thy face?" (Josh. 7:10). God had something for Joshua to do; his time for crying was over.

When God sent the men of Israel into Jericho, He told them to kill every man, woman, and child. He also told them that "all the silver, and gold, and vessels of brass and iron, are consecrated unto the LORD: they shall come into the treasury of the LORD" (Josh. 6:19). What Joshua didn't know was that these instructions concerning the spoils were not followed. God told Joshua that Israel had sinned and that it was his responsibility to rid Israel of "the accursed thing," which they had stolen. It was this sin of covetousness that caused God's wrath to fall on Israel at Ai. So God told Joshua to quit crying and assemble the elders together to find the source of the problem.

Joshua obeyed God and soon found out that Achan was the guilty one. He had taken a Babylonian garment, two hundred shekels of silver, and a wedge of gold that was to be offered to God. As a result, Achan and his entire family were stoned and burned. God removed His wrath from Israel and restored His blessing. After that, the Israelites defeated Ai swiftly.

We often make the mistake in our prayers of talking too much and not listening enough. After we pray about something for a while and nothing happens, or things even get worse, we develop an attitude like Joshua's. We start blaming God, maybe not audibly, but in our own thinking. We look at other people and ask God why He doesn't bless us the same way He blesses them.

Instead of complaining, we need to ask God why we are defeated; then we should be quiet and listen. When we give God the opportunity, He will show us what to do.

A young man came into my office one morning to talk to me about which seminary he should attend. As we talked, I asked him when he felt God called him to the ministry. He said he felt that God wanted him to preach about three years ago. He told his wife what he felt God wanted him to do, and they were both excited about entering the ministry together.

Soon after that he was given a raise at work. God blessed in other ways as well to aid him in his change of vocation. But instead of immediately following up God's call with some action, he kept praying about it. He said that he knew he should've taken some steps to prepare for the ministry, but he didn't.

Then the blessings ceased and the man felt pressure from God to get on with it. But instead he stalled for three years. Finally the pressure was too much and he headed out to do what he knew God wanted him to do.

There will be times when we come to the Lord with a situation and God will say, "When you correct this relationship, or when you pay this debt, or when you obey Me in this area, then I will bless you." Usually what He shows us has nothing to do with our prayer request. For example, what did one wedge of gold from Jericho have to do with a victory at Ai? In one sense nothing, but in God's eyes it was worth the lives of thirty-six soldiers. It may be the way you run your business, a habit, or something you do not even consider wrong, but God has told you it has to go.

In these situations we usually keep on praying. We may even thank God for His forgiveness. We hope that if we pray enough about it, God will let the matter slide. Instead of courageously taking action, we avoid the situation.

The longer we wait, however, the longer God withholds His blessings. God is saying to us, "Why don't you quit complaining about your circumstances and get this thing straightened out?" Sometimes we aren't sure what the problem is. But if we honestly allow God to search our hearts, the problem usually becomes evident.

For example, let's say that in your past you borrowed money from someone and did not pay him back. Sometimes in your prayers this debt looms up before you. Your response may be, "Lord, I know You know about that, and I want to thank You for forgiving me." But it keeps coming back. God saying that though you are forgiven, there is still restitution to be made. God is waiting for you to deal with the unpaid debt; then He will restore His hand of blessing on you

We need to see the big picture—God's big picture. He is not concerned about the money you owe someone or your apologizing to someone for something you may not even remember. But He *is* concerned about your obedience to the initial prompting of His Spirit. He is concerned about how long it takes you to obey Him once you know the truth. Delay is quiet rebellion, and rebellion is sin. To continue praying about something and at the same time refusing to do what you know to be right is covering a rebellious spirit with a cloak of false humility. It is sin (James 4:17).

Importance of Timing

This story of Joshua brings up five principles that we should keep in mind. First, there is a time to wait and a time to act. The time to wait is when we don't know what God wants us to do. The time to act is the moment God shows us what to do and how to go about it.

We Can't Blame God

Second, we should remember that blaming God for our problems is a waste of time. When we find ourselves even slightly shifting the blame to God, it is time for reevaluation. God will allow certain difficulties to surround us, but always with our best interests at heart. When we become critical of our circumstances, we become critical of God. And when we become critical of Him, we are putting more faith in *our* wisdom than in His. This is how we lose sight of God's big picture.

A man named Chuck was losing his business when he came to talk to me about it. In the course of our conversation, I advised him to read Proverbs and to apply the principles that deal with business. Then we both agreed that he should tithe his income.

About one month later, Chuck came to see me again. His business was booming and everything seemed to be going his way. He was praising the Lord and giving Him all the glory for what had happened.

Three months after that, Chuck's business fell apart again—this time worse than before. He quit going to church, he quit tithing, and he refused to pick up the Bible. According to his wife, Chuck blamed the whole mess on God. Things were worse than ever around the house, and there seemed to be no hope for change.

Then one day in the midst of all the disappointment and heartache, Chuck realized what was happening. He admitted to his wife that the Lord had asked him to give up a certain habit and that he had refused. He said he knew that his problems were his own fault and that he had been wrong in blaming God.

We May Not See a Relationship

Third, we should remember that the thing we need to correct might not even relate to what we are praying about. Since this is true, if we are not honest with ourselves, we will conclude, "This does not even relate to my present circumstances. Surely this is not from the Lord." But if the same thing keeps coming up time after time, you can rest assured it *is* from God—regardless of how long ago it happened.

Chuck couldn't see how his financial problem related to his bad habit. But his financial collapse was God's way of getting his attention. When Chuck saw what God was doing, he quit blaming Him and straightened up.

Late Obedience Is Disobedience

Fourth, we must deal with these issues immediately. Late obedience is disobedience. God is not interested in our prayers when we use them to stall Him. If we ask the Lord, He will show us what needs to be done. Not only that, He will give us explicit directions as to how and when to carry them out. But on receiving His directions, we must act.

Blessing Follows Obedience

Fifth, we can expect God's blessing to follow our obedience to His commands. For Israel, the conquest of Ai followed—not preceded—the stoning of Achan. God's blessing is often dependent on our obedience.

Perhaps as you have read this chapter God has reminded you of something that you need to deal with. It may relate to your family, your job, or your friends. But whatever it is, God wants you to deal with it because He wants the best for you. When He points out something in your life, it is with a finger of love attached to the hand that bears the mark of that love, a nail print. One of the primary reasons many of God's people are not greatly blessed is because they will not get up off their faces and deal with the attitude or action that God has exposed as disobedience.

Continuous prayer without dealing with the point of divine conflict will cheat us out of the success God desires for us in our prayer lives. Nothing is more valuable than unhindered communication with God the Father. As He shines His searchlight of love into your life, will you deal with that which He exposes as foreign to His will for your life? Will you deal with it now?

9

PRAYING FOR OTHERS

I exhort therefore, that, first of all, supplications, prayers,
intercessions, and giving of thanks, be made for all men; For kings,
and for all that are in authority; that we may lead a quiet and
peaceable life in all godliness and honesty. For this is good and
acceptable in the sight of God our Saviour; Who will have all men
to be saved, and to come unto the knowledge of the truth. For there
is one God, and one mediator between God and men, the man
Christ Jesus; Who gave himself a ransom for all, to be testified in
due time. Whereunto I am ordained a preacher, and an apostle, (I
speak the truth in Christ, and lie not;) a teacher of the Gentiles in
faith and verity. I will therefore that men pray every where, lifting
up holy hands, without wrath and doubting. —1 Timothy 2:1–8

All of us have had the frustrating experience of praying for others
and seeing no results. We blame it on our lack of faith or on some

unknown sin in our lives. But often the real problem is that we aren't aware of what the Bible teaches about praying for others. Scripture makes it clear that when we pray for others, certain principles should be followed. It is important that we understand and apply these principles if we are going to see God meet the needs and make the necessary changes in the lives of those for whom we pray. But let's take a closer look at the people the Bible instructs us to pray for.

Those in Authority

Paul says that we are to pray for kings and all those in authority (1 Tim. 2:2). For us, that would mean our president, our congress, our mayors, and even our bosses. We are to intercede on their behalf, taking their needs to the Lord. Then we are to give thanks for them.

The moral decline in America, corruption in high places, loss of credibility among our leaders, and loss of faith in them require renewed commitment on our part to pray for our leaders.

We should pray that every person who runs for public office, as well as those appointed, would fear God and acknowledge Him as Lord. With ungodly men in authority, how can we "lead a quiet and peaceable life in all godliness and honesty" (1 Tim. 2:2)? Ungodly leadership creates conflict and strife. The writer of Proverbs declares, "When the righteous are in authority, the people rejoice: but when the wicked beareth rule, the people mourn" (Prov. 29:2).

Paul exhorts us to pray (1 Tim. 2:1). The word *exhort* means to encourage strongly. We are strongly encouraged to pray for the men and women in public office. We should pray they will see the problems that plague our society from God's point of view. If ever there was an admonition that needs to be heeded by God's people, it is this word from Paul to pray for those in authority.

The Body of Christ

Next, we are to pray for the body of Christ—the church. We are responsible for praying for all the saints (Eph. 6:18). One part of the body of Christ is under persecution. Another part is lukewarm. Another part is cold, having set aside the truth of the Word of God and doubting its authenticity. Still another part of the body is in financial need. We are to intercede for each part according to its specific needs, not just toss out a general request such as, "Bless the church." We are to pray for *all* the saints, not just the group we are personally involved with.

Vocational Servants

We should also pray for God's servants—those who have been called into full-time service. In a sense, we are all full-time servants. But we should particularly pray for those who have made spiritual service their life vocations—pastors, teachers, missionaries, and evangelists.

Paul tells us how. First, we are to pray that utterance would be given; that is, we are to pray that God would show His servants what to preach and teach. Second, we are to pray that these special servants would speak the truth boldly. Then, we are to pray that they would make known the mystery of the gospel—that their message would be clear. These are three specifics Paul knew from personal experience to be the keys to an effective ministry.

As a pastor, there is nothing more reassuring than to know that people are praying for me. There is an elderly, semi-invalid preacher in our church who gets up at 2:00 every morning to pray for me. Occasionally he sends me verses dealing with the specific needs the Lord has laid on his heart concerning my life. He is always right on target, and his letters and verses are always an encouragement.

For pastors, no asset is more precious than the consistent prayers of God's people. However, one major problem in the church today is that people spend more time *criticizing* their pastors than they do *praying* for them. More than ever, God's servants need to be upheld in prayer. More than ever they need utterance, boldness, and clarity in presenting the gospel. It is time we stopped criticizing and started interceding.

Laborers

We are to pray for the laborers, the people yet to be called. Jesus challenged His disciples, "Pray ye therefore the Lord of the harvest, that he will send forth labourers into his harvest" (Matt. 9:38). We are to pray for those whom God calls to heed His call and go forth in His power preaching, teaching, singing, and taking places of leadership in the church.

There are people at this very moment struggling with God's call to enter the ministry. The enemy is doing all in his power to draw them into the world. These people need our prayers, especially to bind Satan's powers from influencing their decisions. We need to pray that they will be sensitive and obedient to the promptings of the Spirit.

The Lost

Likewise, we are to pray for the lost. The vast majority of Scriptures relating to prayer admonish us to pray for the saints. But Paul also tells us that it is God's will for everyone to be saved (1 Tim. 2:4–6). To pray for the lost is to pray in accordance with God's will.

Our Enemies

There is one last group we are to pray for: our enemies. Jesus said, "Love your enemies, bless them that curse you, do good to them that hate you, and pray for them which despitefully use you, and persecute you" (Matt. 5:44). It is often difficult to pray for those we don't like, especially if they feel the same way toward us. So why are we instructed to pray for our enemies? For the same reason we are to pray for everyone else: in order "that we may lead a quiet and peaceable life in all godliness and honesty" (1 Tim. 2:2). The point is this: None of these prayers are to be based on personal likes or dislikes, but rather on our desire for peace and godliness for all mankind.

One result of placing godly men in office and praying for them is a peaceful and godly society. In the same way, praying for our authority at home or work will result in peace in those places. God may bring peace by first working in us, but regardless of how He does it, He promises the end result will be the same.

Through prayer, God closes gaps created by conflict. He then manifests His Spirit of godliness and reverence. Peace and godliness in our homes, our nations, and our jobs depend on our prayers. I am convinced that if God's people will pray the way God intended, He will work a miracle in this country. There will be a quietness and peace this generation has never known.

However, if we fail to pray, our society will continue to spiral downward into chaos. God's people are responsible. For only we have access to almighty God—the Source of power who is able to change this degenerating condition.

How to Pray

Now that we understand whom we are to pray for, let's find out how to pray for them. Too often we pray for others to appease our consciences, and not with the intent or expectation of change. We pray vague prayers with no specific blessings in mind. If we are going to pray, let's learn to pray effectively.

A Heart of Compassion

We must keep in mind that we are to pray from hearts of love and compassion. God will ignore prayers that have the slightest hint of prejudice or anger. And besides, we will not pray consistently for people toward whom we feel resentment and bitterness. Regardless of what was done or who was to blame, God wants our attitudes right when we pray.

We are not to live our lives reacting to others, but rather responding to His Spirit. If we are willing for God to heal our bitterness toward our enemies, He will do it. Many times He will do it through our prayers for them. Whatever the case, we must pray from hearts filled with love and compassion.

Prayer Is the Link

Next, we must realize that our prayers are the link between God's inexhaustible resources and people's needs. Through prayer we direct God's hand of infinite resources to the hand of the person in need. God is the Source of power, but we are the instruments He uses to link the two together. We stand in the gap between the need and the satisfaction of that need. When we see ourselves in that position, we will understand the need for consistent, unwavering prayer. We will begin to pray without ceasing.

One afternoon a pastor from another city came by seeking advice about a church problem. A few deacons in his church were trying to run things. They were a real source of irritation, and this pastor had taken as much as he could stand. That evening his church was going to discuss the manner in which deacons were to be selected. These particular men had threatened to challenge the pastor publicly before the whole congregation. They had been successful in getting their way until then, and this pastor knew that it was time to turn things around or the church would really suffer.

He was troubled and fearful. We talked for a while, and I gave him a verse to claim during the business meeting: "I will go in the strength of the Lord GOD: I will make mention of thy righteousness, even of thine only" (Ps. 71:16). Then I told him I would pray. I stood in the gap between the pastor and the victory he needed. I prayed specifically that God would close the mouths of those who would come against my friend as God closed the mouths of the lions in Daniel's case. Late that night he called me back. He was so excited I could hardly understand him. He said that it was the smoothest business meeting they had ever had and that no one said a word in opposition to his proposals.

Sometimes we will be the only person standing in the gap in a given situation. This is especially true if we are the only person who knows of a particular need. Intercession in this case becomes our sole responsibility. This kind of prayer is work, yet it is rewarding. This is how Christ prayed, for He stood in the gap between God and all mankind. He was the link between God and the entire human race. In the same way, we must make ourselves available for the sake of others.

Identify with Their Needs

To pray effectively for others, we must be able to identify with their needs. Spiritually and emotionally, we must feel what they feel. When Jesus looked out over the crowd, He had "compassion on them" (Matt. 20:34; see also 9:36; 14:14; Mark 1:41; Luke 7:13). He felt what they felt. Christ was tempted and tried in every point that we are (Heb. 4:15). Why? One reason was so He could pray effectively for us. He knows how we feel in every situation we face. When you and I talk with the Lord, He can identify with us. He lived at home for thirty years; He knows the problems encountered there. He worked in a carpenter's shop; He can identify with the laborer. He was hated and rejected; He can identify with the downtrodden.

I was able to identify with the pastor who faced the opposition in his church because I had faced a similar situation. As I prayed, I remembered how I had felt when I faced opposition from deacons. I remembered the feelings of rejection. I remembered the pressure I felt every Sunday as I stood to preach. All of this motivated me to pray earnestly for my friend. Identifying with him allowed me to pray in a way that few other people could.

Purpose for Suffering

One primary reason God allows us to suffer is so we can identify with others in our prayers. Until we suffer, we tend to stereotype those who suffer as inferior and weak. We have little patience with them, much less any burden to pray for them. But Christ lived among the rejected and suffering. He was one of them.

When we avoid pain, we limit our usefulness to God. Through the comfort we receive in our trials, we learn to comfort others (2 Cor. 1:4). This verse implies that if we have never needed comforting, we won't know how to comfort others.

So if we are going to pray for others, we must ask the Lord to help us see what others see ... to feel what they feel. We must understand their hurts. And the only way to do that is to experience hurt ourselves. When we share in another's pain, we will pray with an earnestness we have never known before.

Desire the Best for Others

As we pray for others, we must desire their highest good. We must die to all selfish desires concerning them and seek only God's best. We can put no conditions on God in our prayers—no matter what the cost to us. For example, if a girl is praying for her boyfriend to be saved, she must be willing to do anything for God to answer her prayer. If she says, "I'll do anything but break up with him," then God may only answer her prayer on the condition that she become willing to break up. When we give God a condition, He often makes *that* the condition on which the answer to our prayer hinges.

Carl had been praying for months about his rebellious son. His twenty-two-year-old son had left home and was living with some boys in a shack outside of town. My friend knew his son had been involved with drugs before he left home and soon after learned that his son had become a drug dealer. Carl's two main concerns were that God would bring his son home and that his son wouldn't be arrested.

One morning while he was praying for his son, God spoke to Carl. Carl realized that this had been a selfish request. He was well-known in his town and would be embarrassed if his son was arrested on drug charges. Carl told the Lord that if the only way to deliver his son from his sin was to allow him to be arrested, then he was willing for that to happen—even at the expense of his reputation.

A few days later, Carl received a phone call from the police. His son had been arrested and was charged with possession of illegal drugs. As Carl drove to the police station to pick up his son, he realized that God had been waiting for him to get his attitude right before He could allow his son to come home.

God honored Carl's obedience. He and his son rebuilt their broken relationship and soon afterward his son left home again, this time to study for ministry.

When we pray for someone, we must take our hands off the matter completely and let God work *any* way He sees fit. It may not come out the way we want it, but the outcome will always be in the best interest of both parties.

Being Part of the Answer

When praying for others, we must be willing to be part of the answer if necessary. If we aren't willing to be used to answer our own prayers, we aren't cooperating with God. As a result, He won't cooperate with us; He won't answer our prayers. Why? Because these are prayers of isolation and separation. We are saying, "God I don't want to get mixed up in anyone's problems. *You* take care of that."

Can you imagine Jesus doing that? "Sorry, Bartimaeus, I don't want to get *My* hands dirty." God will not hear our prayers of isolation. If we aren't more interested than that, then He's not interested in our prayers. As long as we ask and do nothing, He will listen and do nothing. If it costs us nothing, we can expect little in return.

Don't pray for more missionaries unless you're willing to go yourself or are willing to send your children. Don't pray for another's financial need unless you're willing to give yourself. And don't pray for the lost unless you're willing to go to them and share what Christ means to you.

We Must Persevere

When we intercede for others, we must persevere. We must be willing to keep on praying until the answer comes. One reason we don't see more answers to prayer is because we aren't willing to pay the price; and often the price is *time*. If we are really burdened for someone and are really feeling what he or she feels, we can't possibly stop praying until the burden is lifted. But if we are only praying out of pity or to appease our consciences, we will soon forget the one in need. One true test of loyalty to our friends is if we are willing to lay down our lives for them in prayer. Our faithfulness to our friends can be measured by the consistency of our prayers for them.

We lie when we flippantly say to people, "I love you," and then forget to pray for them in their times of need. Yet how many times has someone asked us to pray about a specific need and we say, "I'll be praying for you"—then we pray for him or her casually, if we remember the prayer request at all? We need to examine ourselves and see if we really know what love is all about. We will pray consistently for those we really love. This is the reason our prayers are so often full of our own desires and needs.

Ask God to show you three people He wants you to pray for—three people who have burdens, heartaches, or specific needs. Tell God you are willing to be part of the answer. Then ask Him to share their burdens with you. Ask God for a real spirit of compassion and love for these three. Tell Him you want Him to teach you how to pray and intercede on their behalf. Start with three and then add as the Lord leads.

If all of us were to start praying for one another, the Spirit of God would release the blessing of heaven on us. Homes would be mended, businesses would be blessed, and churches would be in a constant spirit of revival. There is no way to describe what God would do in your own life if you would apply these simple principles to your prayers. But you will never *be* the same nor *pray* the same again.

10
PRAYER IS WHERE THE ACTION IS

*Then came Amalek, and fought with Israel in
Rephidim. And Moses said unto Joshua, Choose us
out men, and go out, fight with Amalek: to morrow
I will stand on the top of the hill with the rod of
God in mine hand. So Joshua did as Moses had said
to him, and fought with Amalek: and Moses, Aaron,
and Hur went up to the top of the hill. And it came
to pass, when Moses held up his hand, that Israel
prevailed: and when he let down his hand, Amalek
prevailed. But [Moses'] hands were heavy; and they
took a stone, and put it under him, and he sat thereon;
and Aaron and Hur stayed up his hands, the one on
the one side, and the other on the other side; and
his hands were steady until the going down of the
sun. And Joshua discomfited Amalek and his people
with the edge of the sword. —Exodus 17:8–13*

As the children of Israel traveled through the wilderness on their way to Canaan, many who were weak and sick fell to the rear of the caravan and were left to keep up the best way they could. As a result, the Israelites were stretched out many miles through the desert. Amalek, a nomadic tribe of that region, took advantage of this situation and attacked and plundered those who fell behind. So the Israelites were forced to fight even though they were far less prepared for war than the Amalekites. It was no secret that the Israelites had walked out of Egypt loaded down with as much wealth as they could carry. The Amalekites were willing to take any risk to steal this wealth for themselves.

Moses tells Joshua to choose his men and fight the Amalekites (Ex. 17:9). In the meantime, Moses, Aaron, and Hur climbed a hill where they could watch the battle. As the two armies began fighting, Moses raised the rod of God above his head, and the battle immediately turned around; the nation of Israel began to win. When he lowered the rod because of weariness, Amalek began winning the battle. It quickly became apparent to Moses, Aaron, and Hur that the determining factor in this battle was whether or not Moses held up his staff. So Aaron and Hur sat Moses on a rock and each one of them took one of Moses' arms and held it up. And even though the army of Israel was at a disadvantage because of their lack of equipment and preparation, they still defeated the Amalekites.

Where the Battle Is Won

The battle wasn't won because of the army's strength or because of Joshua's military genius. The battle was won on the hilltop as

Aaron and Hur held up the hands of Moses. It was the action on the hilltop that determined the outcome of the action in the valley.

This incident shows us three principles that, if observed carefully, will make our prayer lives more exciting and our prayers more fruitful. First, life's battles are won or lost in the place of prayer, not on the battlefield of everyday life. The real spiritual success or failure of a church does not depend on the talent of the preacher, the size of the congregation, or the strength of the organization. Success from God's point of view will be obtained only through prayer. The person who sees these other things as the criteria for success has no concept of the working of the Holy Spirit. It is by these outward signs that the world judges the church. But God does not win His battles through outward signs. God wins His battles through men and women who intercede on behalf of the kingdom.

There was a time when I dreaded our monthly deacons' meetings. They normally lasted for over three hours, and when we finished, I was drained emotionally and physically because so little was usually accomplished. Then the Lord laid it on one of the deacon's hearts to begin a Saturday morning prayer meeting for the deacons.

Each Saturday we met and prayed for two or three hours. The Lord began to knit our hearts together in an unusual way. There was oneness of mind and purpose among us like there had never been before.

Soon the nature of our monthly meetings changed. The atmosphere was more relaxed and everyone was more agreeable. The meeting time was cut to less than half of what it was before, and everyone agreed that we accomplished more. Business was taken care of so quickly that we moved the meeting time to Sunday afternoon.

The deacons agreed that praying together on Saturday morning made the difference. God's business, for the most part, is to be taken care of on our knees. When dealing with any situation, first we must pray. It is on our knees that the real work is done.

In this incident from the book of Exodus, God wanted to teach Moses, Joshua, and the rest of the people a lesson. There was more going on than just a battle between two armies. A great spiritual battle was happening as well. God's message is this: In our spiritual conflicts, the outcome is not determined by what is seen in the field of battle, but rather by what happens in the place of prayer. That is why throughout the Old Testament God put His people in arenas where they faced overwhelming disadvantages. Then, to the amazement of all who saw or heard, His people proved victorious. Why? Out of a spirit of total dependence on Him and unwavering faith in Him, they fought the real battles on their faces before God. Their public victories were the outcome of their private victories.

As we, in total dependence on God, bow our knees before the conflict begins, God turns our eyes toward Him. He sifts and cleanses us in preparation for the coming battle. God gives us His perspective of the battle, which is always far superior to our own. Our faith soars as we see that those who war against us must also war against the Christ who is within us. He shows us His sufficiency for whatever we are facing. Then He promises us victory by

His own Word. As we rise from our places of prayer, we march into any battle confident of victory. For the battle is the Lord's and the victory is ours. "Now thanks be unto God, which always causeth us to triumph in Christ" (2 Cor. 2:14).

Many conflicts in the home would be brought to quick conclusions if family members would bow before God, search their own hearts, and surrender their battles to Him. We must realize that He alone is the Source of *all* things, spiritual and material (2 Peter 1:3). We must enter into each situation with our total dependence on Him. Then, and only then, will God release His supernatural power to overcome the enemy.

A Lesson Worth Sharing

The lesson Moses learned was so important that God specifically told him to tell Joshua the whole story in detail. God knew that Joshua would soon become the leader of the Israelites. He also knew that through the many battles to be fought, Joshua would need the assurance that God was fighting beside them. God wanted Joshua's perspective of war to be a heavenly perspective. The same must be true for us.

One problem is that we often don't know who the enemy is. We act as if people are our enemies—our families, our bosses, even our friends. But the Bible makes it clear that Satan is our enemy (Eph. 6:12). Satan knew that the Messiah would come through the nation of Israel. The Amalekites and all the other nations that warred with Israel were instruments of Satan—weapons to get at God's people and, in a sense, to get at God.

For the Israelites, the physical conflict was not the real conflict at all. The same is true for conflicts we face today. If we don't fight our battles on our knees, we will mistake all kinds of people for the enemy. While they *appear* to be our enemies, Satan is the ultimate source of our conflicts.

A college student was having trouble getting along with her unsaved father. Regardless of how sweet she was, they just could not get along. She soon found herself becoming bitter. As she prayed, the Lord revealed a strategy to combat her bitterness.

She was to understand that the conflict wasn't between her and her father but rather between Satan and God. She saw that Satan was using her father as an instrument to overcome the Christ in her.

When she adopted this attitude, things at home began to change. She no longer saw her father as her enemy. On the contrary, she saw for the first time how he really loved her. When conflicts would arise, instead of reacting to her father, she would go to her knees in prayer and deal with the real enemy.

As Satan sows seeds of disunity throughout the church, many of God's people find themselves in conflict with each other. These conflicts are usually never resolved because nobody deals with the real enemy—Satan. There is no way to win a battle if we don't know who our enemy is. And because our real enemy is a spiritual being, the only way we can really deal with him is on our knees.

God is the Source of all victory. Through faith in Him and His willingness to fight our battles for us, we can approach life from a standpoint of victory, regardless of the circumstances. This is not a victory claimed and won on the battlefield of life but a victory claimed and won on our knees in private before the public battle ever begins.

We May Become Weary

Second, we must remember that when we face life's battles, we will become weary at times. Even Moses, God's greatest statesman, grew weary as he held the rod of God over his head. Though he started out strong, he soon tired and finally dropped his arms completely. He knew that the raised rod was the key to victory, but he just couldn't keep it up. Just in time, Aaron and Hur sat him down and lifted his arms until the battle was over and the Amalekites were defeated.

In spite of the fact that Jesus told us to pray and not faint (Luke 18:1), we still faint. We lose heart. Sometimes it is because we look at the circumstances around us. Other times, we simply lose the burden. There are also times when Satan warps our perspective to discourage us; we see problems as larger than they really are.

God knows we will grow fainthearted at times. He understands when we feel like giving up. He knows that sometimes we just won't feel like carrying on. But this is where the third principle from this story fits in.

Finding Our Own Aaron and Hur

God sent Moses up to that hill knowing that he couldn't hold up the rod for too long by himself. It was no accident that Aaron and Hur went along. They gave Moses the support he needed.

In the same way, God won't let us be totally independent of others. God has built His church on a system of interdependence, each person ministering to others through their different talents, gifts, abilities, and prayers. But at the same time, everyone recognizes God as the Source of all blessings.

All of us need an "Aaron" and a "Hur": Two people we can share our needs and burdens with. Christ in the garden of Gethsemane revealed His burden. He too needed the prayer support of His friends, but He found them asleep.

Aaron and Hur didn't serve as Moses' counselors. They didn't tell him how to hold the rod so he wouldn't grow tired. They were his supporters. They physically held up the rod by supporting Moses' arms.

All too often, people will give us advice for our spiritual battles, but they won't give of their time in prayer. Who is willing to listen attentively to your hurts and then pray until God lifts the burden? We need less counseling and more praying—for God is moved by Spirit-filled praying, not by good advice. And God is the only One with power enough to win our battles for us.

A Threefold Cord

"A threefold cord is not quickly broken" (Eccl. 4:12). Something supernatural takes place when three believers with genuine concern for one another and unwavering faith in God intercede for one another. God has honored this type of intercession in my life many times. I have had an "Aaron" and a "Hur" who have prayed with me through financial difficulties, family problems, church-related problems, and deep personal hurts. To have two other men get under my burdens with tears on my behalf is one of the most encouraging and strengthening experiences of my spiritual life. It serves as a physical reassurance that God is concerned about my problems. My faith soars in the midst of conflict when I hear the faith-filled prayers of my friends petitioning God on my behalf. And not only does it build my faith, but it builds theirs as well.

There will be times when we have the opportunity to intercede on behalf of the ones who have prayed for us. As love develops between prayer partners, sensitivity to one another's needs also develops. We recognize and feel their hurts without their saying anything; the Spirit reveals to us who needs prayer. When we have two encouraging forces, our faintheartedness turns into courage and confidence, and God's power becomes a reality.

Spiritually Minded

What kind of people should we look for when we ask God to send us an "Aaron" and a "Hur"? First, we should look for those who are:

Spiritually Minded and Actively Seeking God. Look to those who obey and trust the Lord, regardless of the circumstances. Whether or not we think they are as spiritual as we are is not an issue here. It is the condition of their hearts that matters.

Warriors—Not Counselors. Second, we should look for those who accept us as we are, regardless of the problems we may be facing. They must see themselves as sent to lift us up, not criticize us. They must see themselves as prayer warriors, not counselors.

A Compassionate Heart. An "Aaron" and a "Hur" must have compassionate hearts. They must be able to feel what we feel. They need to know what it means to hurt. They must also have a willingness to give of themselves and ask nothing in return—to love us as Christ does, unconditionally and unselfishly.

Faithful. Last of all, our prayer warriors must be faithful. We don't need people who will come only when it is convenient. These people must be willing to come when we need them. They must be willing to stop whatever they are doing and come to our aid in prayer. Something happens in our lives when we have an "Aaron" and a "Hur" standing by our sides, beseeching almighty God on our behalf. There is a new freedom and confidence and also greater spiritual fruitfulness. We must ask ourselves: *Am I the kind of Christian who someone would want as an "Aaron" or a "Hur"? Do I meet the qualifications?*

There is no way for three people to bind themselves together in Christ and pray for one another without growing and becoming stronger in their faith. Among groups like this the real battles in life are fought and won. This is how God intends for all of us to fight our battles—on our faces before Him with others who will pay any price for victory.

What would happen in our families if we became the "Aaron" or "Hur" for our spouses and children? What would happen in our churches and in our businesses if we began praying with people there in the spirit of an "Aaron" and a "Hur"? God must strip us of our pride. He is not going to let us make it alone. He wants us to recognize our need for each other and to unite spiritually.

What About You?

Are you like the nation of Israel—trapped in a valley and facing battles that defeat you time after time? Then you need an "Aaron" and a "Hur." Ask God to develop in you the needed qualities. Then ask Him to send you two others who likewise have prepared themselves for spiritual battles. A threefold cord is not easily broken, and neither is the faith of three people committed to interceding for another in the Spirit's power.

11
THE WARFARE OF PRAYER

Then was brought unto him one possessed with a devil,
blind, and [mute]: and he healed him, insomuch that
the blind and [mute] both spake and saw. And all the
people were amazed and said, Is not this the son of
David? But when the Pharisees heard it, they said, This
fellow doth not cast out devils, but by Beelzebub the
prince of devils. And Jesus knew their thoughts, and
said unto them, Every kingdom divided against itself is
brought to desolation; and every city or house divided
against itself shall not stand: And if Satan cast out
Satan, he is divided against himself; how shall then his
kingdom stand? And if I by Beelzebub cast out devils,
by whom do your children cast them out? Therefore
they shall be your judges. But if I cast out devils by the
Spirit of God, then the kingdom of God is come unto
you. Or else how can one enter into a strong man's

house, and spoil his goods, except he first bind the
strong man? And then he will spoil his house. He that
is not with me is against me; and he that gathereth not
with me scattereth abroad. —Matthew 12:22–30

There is one primary reason we pray weak prayers: We don't comprehend God's promises concerning the release of His supernatural power through prayer. We see prayer as only involving God and our requests, and we miss the big picture.

Paul described what warfare prayer is all about when he wrote, "Finally, my brethren, be strong in the Lord, and in the power of his might. Put on the whole armour of God, that ye may be able to stand against the wiles of the devil" (Eph. 6:10–11). We are entering a war where we will need strength greater than our own. He identifies our enemy, Satan, and commands us to make provision to battle against him by putting on the armor of God.

Then Paul stated the realm and nature of warfare prayer: "For we wrestle not against flesh and blood, but against principalities, against powers, against the rulers of the darkness of this world, against spiritual wickedness in high places" (v. 12).

The Enemy We Face Today

The body of Christ is in constant conflict against spiritual forces. When the church of Jesus Christ was born, it was born in the midst of the heathen empire of Rome. Two thousand years later in

America, the church of the Lord Jesus Christ is again in the midst of a heathen empire. It is a capitalistic empire that is anti-God; it is a system whose religion is humanism. Its philosophy declares that man is sufficient within himself to meet his own needs. The church is surrounded by a system that denies there is a God. Man is his own god.

In the early days, the New Testament church suffered persecution for the truth. As a result, the Roman Empire recognized that the gospel of Jesus Christ was a greater power than the Roman military machine. Christians showed their spiritual power—they believed, they stood, they gave, and they died. And where is the Roman Empire today? For long after the nation of Rome collapsed, the Christian faith continues.

The Challenge

Today in America the body of Christ faces the challenge of humanism. We must decide now if we are going to compromise. Will we close the Word of God? Or will we stand true to what we know is right? Are we willing to pay the price in the twenty-first century for the sake of future generations?

God knows the enemy we would face, and He does not leave us to fight alone. Through the power of prayer, He has equipped us to overcome the forces and influences of humanism. He has given us the power and responsibility to make an indelible impression on our society. But are we willing to do so?

Prayer has always been our most powerful weapon. And yet we as Christians in America have allowed our nation to degenerate into its present condition by our failure to exercise our divinely given authority to pray. Yes, we are responsible! Why? Because America has a spiritual problem and it will take a spiritual answer to solve it.

The Responsibility of the Church

The church has a ministry not only of winning people to Christ but of dealing with all kinds of people, wherever they are spiritually. We combat Satan to rescue people from his bondage and free them to become the men and women God wants them to be. But because of our weakness and lack of faith, the church has recoiled from such warfare. We have concluded that our only task is to lead people to Christ and put them on the church roll, but that is far from the total purpose of the church.

There are those who say we are not to get involved with political issues or healing or anything out of the ordinary. Some people teach that healing and casting out demons and many other works of the Holy Spirit ended in the first century. But the responsibility of the body of Christ today is the same as it was two thousand years ago.

Christ said, "Behold, I give unto you power to tread on serpents and scorpions, and over all the power of the enemy: and nothing shall by any means hurt you" (Luke 10:19). The first reference to the word *power* means authority. The second reference means strength. Christ was telling His disciples that He was giving them all the power and strength they needed to overcome all the power and strength of the enemy.

Equipped for the Task

If Christ has given us a responsibility today equal to the responsibility of Christians two thousand years ago, it only makes sense that He has equipped us with the same power for the task. We have been saved and are being sanctified for the purpose of glorifying God. To glorify Him, we must obey Him. To obey Him, we must take to heart the Great Commission—and go!

Every believer is to carry out Christ's commission in whatever way possible. For two thousand years, men and women have been going out as a result of Christ's command. We are the fruits of their labor. Each of us has the same responsibility.

God has given the present-day church the same amount of authority and power over satanic forces as He did the first-century church. Since this is true, we have the same responsibility as the early church had to bind the prince of this earth and reclaim for God what is rightfully His.

There is only one omnipotent Being on the earth—almighty God. Satan is *not* omnipotent; he is merely a fallen angel. But the church acts as if Satan is omnipotent. We treat Satan as if he has equal power with God. We often think of him as just a little less powerful than God. We continue to retreat while Satan advances.

Through Christ, God made His major attack against Satan. Christ's death and resurrection gave us victory over the consequences and the power of sin. Through Christ, we have overcome Satan; he has been conquered. Now God sends us, indwelt by His Spirit and supernaturally endowed, to conquer Satan. We are to reclaim for God the lives of men and women who are in bondage to sin. We are God's ambassadors to a lost and dying world (2 Cor. 5:20).

But we will accomplish this great work only when we get our eyes off our past failures and set them on God and His Word. We must begin to appropriate what is ours, instead of allowing the supernatural power of God to lie dormant within us.

Once some Pharisees were accusing Jesus of casting out demons in the name of Satan (Matt. 12:24). So Christ said, "Look, do you think Satan would cast out his own demonic powers and divide his own kingdom? If I am casting out demons in the name of God, then the kingdom of God has come to your doorsteps, and you do not even recognize it" (see vv. 26–28). This was the worst accusation Jesus could have made, seeing them as the very ones who were to identify the Messiah when He came.

The Essence of Spiritual Warfare

Jesus summed up the essence of spiritual warfare by saying, "How can one enter into a strong man's house, and spoil his goods, except he first bind the strong man? And then he will spoil his house" (Matt. 12:29). Christ again mentioned this idea of binding: "I will give unto thee the keys of the kingdom of heaven: and whatsoever thou shalt bind on earth shall be bound in heaven: and whatsoever thou shalt loose on earth shall be loosed in heaven" (16:19). Spiritual warfare is binding and loosing according to the leading of the Holy Spirit.

We are living in conflict with the world, a conflict that will continue until Jesus comes. We are all involved in one way or another, whether we like it or not. We will be either an asset or a hindrance to the army of God. We will be either a victor or a captive.

Paul makes it clear that we are not coming against people or circumstances in this war, for Satan and his host are our enemy (Eph. 6:11–12). This is a spiritual conflict, and therefore, we must be spiritually prepared. We must have on the *whole* armor of God. And if we are going to put it on, we must understand what it is.

Loins Girded with Truth

First, we are to have our loins girded with truth. This means more than just reading the Word; we must understand exactly what it says and who it says we are. We must understand our position in Christ and His position in us. By faith we must see that the battleground is in the heavenlies—the real struggle is between God and Satan.

The holes in our theology are where Satan builds his strongholds. Our wrong perspective of spiritual things often leaves us ineffective when it comes to warfare prayer. *Having* the truth is not enough. We must *know* the truth if we are to be set free (John 8:32). We must have our loins girded about with the knowledge and application of the truth if we are to be truly prepared for battle.

The Breastplate of Righteousness

Next, we are to wear the breastplate of righteousness. This doesn't mean righteous acts. Instead, it means we are to accept God's gift of righteousness (Rom. 5:17). We have already been made the righteousness of God in Christ (2 Cor. 5:21). To be prepared for battle, we must accept that gift of righteousness.

This is hard for most people to do. We aren't taught to think of ourselves as righteous. But it all goes back to the first piece of armor—we must know the truth of God's Word if we are to enter into warfare prayer. When our doctrine is biblically correct, we'll think of ourselves from God's perspective.

The church I attended as a young boy emphasized man's sinfulness. The preacher never mentioned the righteousness we receive when we become Christians. As a result, I grew up feeling condemned by God. I never felt that I could live up to God's expectations of me. This negative teaching made such an impact on me that I spent the first years of my ministry trying to make myself acceptable in God's sight. What a relief it was when I found out that I was acceptable to God just because I was in Christ. I no longer had to worry about what God was thinking about me. In His sight I was righteous. My only responsibility at that moment was to accept His gift of righteousness.

The Bible clearly teaches that in Christ we are righteous. To think of ourselves as anything less is to go into battle without the most important part of our armor—the breastplate. Our wrong thinking in this area allows Satan to make us feel unworthy in God's presence. "Who are you to expect God to answer your prayer?" he asks. There is only one answer. "I am the righteousness of God in Christ, that's who I am!" (see 2 Cor. 5:21).

If God didn't make us as righteous as Christ, how could we get into heaven? Too often we go into battle unprepared. As a result, we neglect our relationship with God because we feel so defeated and unworthy. We must accept God's gift of righteousness as we enter into spiritual warfare.

The Preparation of the Gospel of Peace

It is essential that we have our feet prepared with the gospel of peace. The key here is the word *peace*. Paul was referring to the peace we can have in this life. Most of the time we think of the gospel as the promise of heaven if a person accepts Christ as their Savior. But Paul was talking about a new life on this earth as a result of accepting Christ. In other words, we must be prepared to lead others to Christ. The person who enters into warfare prayer must understand the peace that God has provided for us on this earth.

Paul wrote, "I am crucified with Christ: nevertheless I live; yet not I, but Christ liveth in me: and the life which I now live in the flesh I live by the faith of the Son of God, who loved me, and gave himself for me" (Gal. 2:20). This must be a daily experience for real prayer warriors. For peace only comes as we allow Christ to live through us.

This is the side of the gospel our world needs to see. They have *heard* about heaven: It is time they *see* heaven in our homes, our churches, and our offices. People seek wealth because they see the lifestyle of the wealthy, and people seek Christ when they see the true scriptural lifestyle of Christians. When they come, we must be prepared to guide them into this new life in Christ. We must be prepared to be a part of the answer to our prayers for the lost and backslidden.

The Shield of Faith

Then Paul says we are to take the shield of faith. With this piece of armor we are to quench Satan's fiery darts. Every evil that comes against us is from one source—Satan. We must never lose sight of this; otherwise, we will see the instruments of Satan as our enemies and will never deal with him, the root of the problem.

But how does faith defeat Satan's attacks? Satan attacks with lies, and we defend ourselves by believing what God says, regardless of how Satan makes us feel. For example, let's say you are attacked with a feeling of fear. This is a common dart Satan uses. To defeat Satan you simply meet his lie with an affirmation of God's truth. "The Lord has not given me a spirit of fear, but of power and of love and of a sound mind" (see 2 Tim. 1:7).

Our emotions are often Satan's doorways into our minds. By faith we must stop him at the door. Regardless of what our emotions tell us, we must believe God. We may feel unworthy—but it's a lie. We may feel rejected—but it's a lie. We must renew our minds to the true knowledge of who we are (Col. 3:10). By faith we must accept what God says about us. For faith is our protection against Satan's lies.

The Helmet of Salvation

As we enter into warfare prayer, our armor must include the helmet of salvation. This means that we must have the Holy Spirit living inside of us (Eph. 6:18). The helmet covers and protects the mind. This is also the work of the Holy Spirit. We must live in the power and under the direction of the Holy Spirit. Fleshly power and reasoning are worthless in a spiritual conflict (2 Cor. 10:3–5). Therefore, we must submit our minds, wills, and emotions to the authority of God's Spirit (Gal. 5:16, 25).

The Sword of the Spirit

Last, our armor must include the sword of the Spirit—God's Word. Throughout this book we have noted the importance of Scripture in our prayers. The Bible is the anchor of our faith and the source of our authority.

But God's Word has another use in the context of spiritual warfare and warfare prayer. It is a weapon to be used against our adversary—Satan. This weapon won't do us any good if we don't know how to use it. We must direct the Word of God at Satan in a spiritual attack. There are specific Scriptures that deal with specific attacks of Satan. We are to saturate our prayers with these passages. In this way we can bind Satan from our lives and from the lives of others.

The Strategy of Warfare Prayer

Now that we better understand the preparation of the warfare prayer, let's turn our attention to the warring itself. How are we to deal with the enemy in our lives and in the lives of others? We have already said that the essence of spiritual warfare is binding and loosing (Matt. 16:19). But what are we to bind and loose? This question is also answered in Scripture:

> For the weapons of our warfare are not
> carnal, but mighty through God to the

> pulling down of strong holds; Casting
> down imaginations, and every high
> thing that exalteth itself against the
> knowledge of God, and bringing into
> captivity every thought to the obedience
> of Christ. (2 Cor. 10:4–5)

Through warfare prayer, we have the responsibility and power to come against the strongholds Satan has in our lives and in others' lives.

Strongholds

A stronghold is an area of sin that has become part of our lifestyle. It may be a harmful habit (drugs, fornication, smoking), or it may be an attitude (rejection, loneliness, worry, doubt). We use a whole arsenal of rationalizations and speculations to support these habits or attitudes. But the knowledge on which these strongholds are based directly opposes God's truth (2 Cor. 10:5).

Satan pumps us full of lies that secure these strongholds. They may sound like this: "There's really nothing wrong with this music— I don't listen to the words anyway," or, "I just drink a little when I get nervous." And haven't we all said, "The police won't pull me over for going just five miles per hour over the speed limit, so it's okay"?

Our responsibility as Christians is to tear down these strongholds through Spirit-filled prayers. How? There is only one weapon—the sword of the Spirit. We must fight these lies with God's Word. We must fight specific lies with specific truths.

A young woman continuously struggled to discipline her eating habits. She realized it was a stronghold in her life, and she fought to overcome it. First, she pinpointed the subconscious lies she had believed about her problem. She thought she studied better if she snacked. She also thought that every time she felt hungry she *had* to eat. And she told herself that eating helped her handle her emotions better. But all these things were lies from Satan to keep her in bondage.

She accepted God's account of her life as His child. She believed that she was "a new creature" and that her life was hidden with Christ in God (see Col. 3:3). She accepted the fact that she was not under the dominion of her flesh and its drives (Gal. 5:24).

Then she took portions of Scripture, like these mentioned, and memorized them. Every time she was tempted to eat when she knew she really didn't need to, she met Satan's lies with God's Word. She was consistently victorious from then on.

In our lives we need only ask God in faith to tear down a stronghold, and He will do it. Then we must immediately renew that part of our minds with the true knowledge of God's Word (Rom. 12:2). If we don't, we will be subject to the same lies again and again.

For example, say you have a stronghold of self-condemnation. That is, after you sin and ask God to forgive you, you don't *feel* forgiven. You mope around under a cloud of guilt until you feel sufficient time has passed and your fellowship with the Father can be restored.

To find victory, you must ask God to tear down this stronghold. Name it out loud. Rebuke the lies that Satan has used against you, and tell God that you now accept the truth of His Word. A good Scripture to claim would be Romans 8:1. Also, study God's forgiveness in Scripture. This will focus your attention on the truth. Then, as you meditate on the truth, your mind will respond in a positive way.

Warring for the Saints

This principle of overcoming strongholds can be applied as we pray for other saints as well. But at some point in time, others must take the responsibility for renewing their own minds—we cannot do it for them. We can pray that God will tear down a specific stronghold in their lives, and He will do it. But if they don't rebuke the lies that protected that stronghold, the stronghold will come back. Only application of the truth can stand against Satan's lies.

One evening I shared with my son that God had shown me a stronghold of fear in my life. He smiled and said that the Lord had revealed this problem in my life to him the week before. He had been praying that God would tear down this stronghold and show me my need to renew my mind to the truth in this area. We both went away with a new appreciation for the power of prayer and for God's willingness to tear down our strongholds if we will only let Him.

When we pray for others, we must persist until God reveals to them the truths concerning their strongholds. We must pray that God will convict them of their sins and guide them into the truth. We must claim Christ's promise: "Howbeit when he, the Spirit of truth, is come, he will guide you into all truth: for he shall not speak of himself; but whatsoever he shall hear, that shall he speak: and he will [show] you things to come" (John 16:13). The key is to pray continually. This is why our little "bless him or her" prayers really do no good. We need *specific* truths to combat *specific* strongholds.

Strongholds and the Lost

The lost are also in bondage to strongholds. Strongholds such as procrastination, immorality, self-righteousness, and doubt keep people from experiencing the new life available in Christ. We must ask God to show us what the specific strongholds are. We can then, by the authority invested in us by God, ask God to convict people of their strongholds.

Satan uses lies to keep lost people lost and Christians in bondage. Only through prevailing prayer do we have the hope and freedom that Christ offers. We must bind the spirits of deceit and loose the ministering spirits of truth (Heb. 1:14). This type of prayer sets in motion God's power in such a way that the demons tremble.

Paul wrote, "We wrestle not against flesh and blood" (Eph. 6:12). It is time we quit struggling against flesh and blood and deal with the *real* enemy. We have only one weapon. It is not preaching, teaching, singing, or organizing; it is the Word of God brought against Satan's lies through prayer. Our prayers build the kingdom of God and destroy the kingdom of Satan. But where there is no prayer, there is no warfare. Where there is no warfare, there is no spiritual reality. Where there is no spiritual reality, there is no victory. Where there is no victory, there is nothing glorifying to God.

Christ said, "I glorified You on the earth, having accomplished the work which You have given Me to do" (John 17:4 NASB). We, like Christ, are to glorify the Father. But if we don't enter into the warfare of prayer, we will never fulfill God's plan for our lives. If we don't pray, we serve no purpose in God's framework of eternity.

STUDY GUIDE
A THIRTEEN-SESSION
GROUP LEADER'S GUIDE

General Preparation

Survey the entire text of both *Handle with Prayer* and this Leader's Guide. Underline important passages in the text and make notes as you read. Become familiar with the entire study before you begin. A general knowledge of what is coming up later will enable you to conduct each session more effectively and to keep discussion relevant to the subject at hand. If a group member asks a question that will be considered later in the course, postpone discussion until that time.

Keep in mind that the outline for each session assumes that group members are reading *Handle with Prayer* before each class or group meets.

Add to your teaching notes any material and ideas you think are important to your group. As teacher, your enthusiasm for the

subject and your personal interest in those you teach can determine the interest and response of your group.

We recommend that you plan to use some kind of visual aid,
even if you merely jot down answers to group questions on a chalkboard, whiteboard, or pad of paper on an easel. This will impress
each point on your group. Then make sure *all* the necessary material or equipment is on hand *before* group time.

Encourage group members to bring Bibles or New Testaments
to the meetings and use them during the group time.

Getting Started Right

Start on time. This is especially important for the first session for
two reasons. First, it will set the pattern for the rest of the course.
If you begin the first lesson late, members will have less reason for
being on time at the other sessions. Those who are punctual will be
robbed of time, and those who are habitually late will come even
later next time. Second, the first session should begin promptly
because getting acquainted, explaining the procedure, and intro-
ducing the book will shorten your study time as it is.

Begin with prayer by asking the Holy Spirit to open hearts and
minds, to give understanding, and to apply the truths that will be
studied. The Holy Spirit is the great Teacher. No teaching, however
orthodox and carefully presented, can be truly Christian or spiritual without His control.

Involve everyone. The suggested plans for each session require
participation from the members of your group. This is important
because:

1. People are usually more interested if they take part.

2. People remember more of what they discuss together than they do of what they are told by a lecturer.

3. People like to help arrive at conclusions and applications. They are more likely to act on truth if they apply it to themselves than if it is applied to them by someone else.

4. To promote relaxed involvement, you may find it wise to:

   a. Ask the group to sit in a circle or semicircle. Some who are not used to this idea may feel uncomfortable at first, but the arrangement makes group members feel more at home. It will also make discussion easier and more relaxed.

   b. Remain seated while you teach (unless the group numbers and/or venue will require standing).

   c. Be relaxed in your own attitude and manner. Remember that the group is not "yours" but the Lord's, so don't get tense!

   d. Use some method to get the group better acquainted, unless everyone already knows one another. At the first meeting or two each member could wear a large-lettered name tag. Each person might also briefly tell something about himself or herself, and perhaps tell what, specifically, he or she expects to get from this study.

Adapting the Course

This material is designed for quarterly use on a weekly basis, but it may be readily adapted to different uses. Those who wish to teach the course over a twelve- or thirteen-week period may simply follow the outline, using or excluding review/examination sessions or questions as desired.

For ten sessions, the leader could easily combine four of the shorter lessons into two. The same procedure could be followed for a five-session small group. However, if the material is to be covered in five sessions, each one may last up to two hours with a ten-minute break near the middle. Divide the text chapters among the sessions as needed. Also note that chapter 9 is spread over two sessions; if necessary for scheduling purposes, those could be combined into one session.

SESSION 1
UNVEILING THE HIDDEN
CHAPTER 1

Session Goals

1. To assess our individual prayer lives to see if we really expect God to answer our prayers.

2. To take a long look at our ideas of what God is like, how He feels about people, and what He is willing to do for them.

3. To determine to say yes to whatever God requires of us.

Preparation

1. As you read *Handle with Prayer*, jot down the main kernels of truth in each chapter. Then study chapter 1.

2. Plan your session time carefully to include the Bible teaching about prayer, which should lead into the practicing of prayer in the session.

3. Assemble any teaching tools: whiteboard or chalkboard, markers or chalk.

Discussion

1. Help people get acquainted by asking each member to turn to the person next to him or her and to sum up his or her prayer philosophy in ten words or less. End with the question: "Do you agree?" Partners respond with his or her own thinking on prayer. Don't ask group members to aim for theological definitions, just responses from their personal experiences. Expect negative as well as positive philosophies, since these sessions are expected to clear up misconceptions about prayer as well as give positive insights—all from the Word.

   After this short exercise, point out that no matter what our present philosophies of prayer are, we all want to learn to pray effectively. But we won't learn how unless we obey God's instructions (as opposed to our own reactions, ideas, experiential knowledge) and respond to Him according to His will.

2. Ask the group to turn to Jeremiah 33:1–3. Explain: "The Babylonians were coming toward Jerusalem from the east. They had already defeated the Assyrians, so the people of Jerusalem

knew they didn't stand much of a chance against such a superior military power. The leaders of Jerusalem believed they should align with the Egyptians. But Jeremiah told them, 'God says you are going into captivity. What you really ought to do is believe God, go out, and surrender to the Babylonians.'"

The outraged leaders, thinking Jeremiah was a traitor, threw him in prison and refused to listen to his warning. Jeremiah probably wasn't too surprised at the leaders' reaction. But what would God say to him now? He had obeyed the Lord, and he was in prison because of it—what next?

Why do you think God reaffirmed His identity to Jeremiah (v. 2)? What three prayer principles did He give Jeremiah (v. 3)? Discuss.

3. Explain that Jeremiah was in a real prison. We may be in figurative ones constructed out of circumstances or predicaments, but the bars are just as strong and the walls just as high.

When we are in our prisons, how do we usually pray? Discuss.

According to Scripture, Jeremiah didn't ask God for anything. Rather, he waited to see what God had to say to him.

If we're in our prisons because God needs to get our attention to teach us lessons, what is the quickest way to get out? Discuss.

Deliverance comes as we examine our hearts to find what God wants to teach us. When we learn our lessons, He will free us. Nothing is too hard for Him.

What should we do if we cannot identify God's purpose in a particular trial? Why is waiting on God so difficult? Discuss.

4. *Does God always answer our prayers?* Discuss the three ways God answers: yes, no, or wait. *Do you agree: "God will always answer yes, if we are living right"?* God is sovereign. He answers depending on what He knows is best for us.

   How do we sometimes try to manipulate Him into saying yes? Sometimes we think: *If I do* this, *then God will do* that. Or we plead a verse of Scripture that seems on target for our case and hope God will change His mind.

   Why does God sometimes say no? Remind the group that the whole purpose of Christianity is to glorify God through our submissive obedience to His desires. He says no when it's for our best interest (Rom. 8:28). God is more interested in our character, future, and sanctification than in our momentary gratification.

   When God says wait, what choice does He give us? What do our responses to God's answers reveal about us?

5. What two things does God always want to show us when we seek to know His will? Refer to Philippians 3:7–8 and John 15:16. How does God show us what He is able and willing to do? Answers might come through His Word, through our own experiences, and through the experiences of others.

   What is the one condition God's unveiling rests on? Why is submission necessary?

6. Explain: "If we hear these truths and don't practice them, we become like the person who wants to learn to drive a car

without ever sitting in the driver's seat. The person reads the training manual, learns all the rules of the road, but never actually sits behind the wheel."

We want to move prayer into the reality of our present circumstances. During our times together, we will be using different prayer methods: silent prayers, group prayers, volunteer prayers, written prayers, etc. Today because of the nature of the subject, we will use silent individual prayers.

7. If God has seemed silent to you about something you have prayed for a long time, examine your heart. *Are you harboring unconfessed sin?* If you will submit now, you will move quickly into the attitude in which God will unfold for you some of the things you need to know.

Are you facing a decision that is too big for you to handle? Have you gone through some difficulty that has left you confused and disheartened? Read Jeremiah 33:3 again. Seek God's face, understand who He is, and believe He will clear away all the mist that surrounds your circumstances.

Are you willing to say yes to whatever He requires of you?

8. Spend time in silent prayer as individuals open up their hearts to God. Close with an appropriate prayer of submissive victory.

Activities Before Next Session

1. Read chapter 2.

2. Carve out time for self-evaluation in God's presence. Some suggestions:

   a. Tell God how you really feel about Him, how your prayer life has been, and what changes you're willing to make for Him.

   b. Meditate on Jeremiah 33:1–3, committing yourself wholly to God and believing He is delivering you from your prison.

   c. Keep a small notebook during these sessions in which you record significant insights God shows you from His Word, prayer requests, God's answers (yes, no, or wait).

3. Ask for four volunteers to prepare a talk-show type discussion for next week answering this question: *Why is the church so powerless today?* If no one volunteers, you may assign this task to four members and work with them as they prepare for the discussion.

SESSION 2
PRAYING WITH AUTHORITY
CHAPTER 2

Session Goals

1. To clarify what it means to pray with authority according to Scripture.

2. To examine ourselves to see if we qualify to pray with authority.

3. To pay the price necessary to make praying with authority an integral part of our prayer lives.

Preparation

1. Study chapter 2 of *Handle with Prayer*. Are you praying with authority concerning your members and this session?

2. Check with the four members who prepared the talk-show discussion. They should be ready to share this discussion during this session.

3. Prepare a copy of the Bible study questions (see question 2 below) for the group just in case they don't have the book with them.

Discussion

1. *Have you ever heard anyone pray with genuine authority so that some force of evil was bound or something unusual took place?* If anyone in the group has experienced this, ask them to tell the group about the incident. What was the effect on the observers?

    Don't be surprised if no one can give an example. Simply move on to the next segment of the session.

    Brainstorm with the group and ask them what it means to pray with authority. Record their responses on the chalkboard/whiteboard (if you have one) without commenting. Clarification will come during the session.

2. Divide members into two groups.

    Let each group appoint a leader for the discussion and assign one group to be "group 1" and the other to be "group 2." Have each group take on the following assignments.

Group 1: Study 1 Kings 18:17–39 using these questions: *What was the issue to be decided? How was the Lord's reputation at stake if Elijah's prayer bombed? What was significant about Elijah's prayer of authority? How would you define a prayer of authority?*

Group 2: Study 2 Chronicles 20:1–11 using these questions: *What was the danger that threatened God's people? How was the Lord's reputation at stake if Jehoshaphat's prayer bombed? What was significant about King Jehoshaphat's prayer of victory? How would you define a prayer of authority?*

Allow eight to ten minutes for the groups to discuss their questions. Then ask both groups to report on their answers to the questions.

3. On the chalkboard or whiteboard draw a line down the middle and write down the words *Ineffectual Prayers* over one column, and the words *Prayers of Authority* over the other column. Ask the two groups to compare and contrast ineffectual prayers and prayers of authority. If you don't have a chalkboard or whiteboard, take notes as each group reads their answers—and then reread them to everyone. Discuss.

4. *What confidence did the disciples have when Jesus sent them out in Matthew 28? Why are we so often ineffective and frustrated in our prayer lives?*

Often we grow ineffective and frustrated in our prayer lives because we don't apply the power and authority Christ made available to us.

5. *Why does Satan put such a high priority on destroying our prayer lives?* Refer to Ephesians 6:12. Discuss how our greatest spiritual work is done on our knees.

   How can a believer prepare for this spiritual battle against Satan? Explain that we prepare for battle by putting on all the armor God has provided. Prayer is not rushing into God's presence, asking Him for a few things quickly, and dashing out again. Prayer is a battle. It is in prayer that spiritual battles are won and lost. Refer to Ephesians 6:13–17.

   What two areas does Satan attack in our prayer lives? He attacks our concentration and our faith. *What are some of the lies that Satan uses to make our prayers ineffective?*

6. Ask the previously contacted members to present their talk-show discussion of the question: *Why is the church so powerless today?*

   In conclusion, bring out Dr. Stanley's definitive statements (if the group did not) in the last two paragraphs before the heading "Our Relationship" in chapter 2.

7. Why must we have a right relationship with God through Christ? How can we know God's thoughts? Refer to 1 Corinthians 2:11–12. Why is this an important prerequisite for praying with authority? If we are praying in agreement with God about

something, we know it is just a matter of time until He will bring it about.

Why is a pure heart necessary to pray with authority? Sin means divided loyalty, and God will not trust His authority and power to anyone who is not completely yielded to Him.

How does Satan attempt to use confessed sin against us so that we won't pray with authority? Satan wants to lead us on a guilt trip that will keep us from praying with authority. But we don't go to God in our own righteousness. Our righteousness is from God on the basis of faith (Phil. 3:9).

What is the key to praying with pure motives? We must be committed to living our lives for God's glory *before* we pray.

8. Challenge the group and yourself with the question: *Am I willing to pay the price necessary to pray with authority?* Give members a few moments to silently review the notes they made during the last session. Remind them that submission is the key to effective prayer.

9. Divide members into small prayer groups or pair them off— whichever method seems most appropriate for your group. Ask them to pray with authority concerning their personal needs, needs of the local churches represented, and needs of the universal body of Christ (based on insights gained from the talk-show type discussion).

Activities Before Next Session

1. Read chapter 3.

2. Suggest that each member set aside time every day in the coming week to pray with authority concerning their needs.

SESSION 3
PRAYING AND FASTING
CHAPTER 3

Session Goals

1. To investigate the biblical approach to fasting and praying.

2. To identify needs that would respond to praying and fasting.

3. To determine whether we will make these disciplines part of our lives and act on our resolutions.

Preparation

1. Read and study chapter 3 of *Handle with Prayer*.

2. Bring enough 3" x 5" cards and pencils for everyone.

Discussion

1. Define fasting. Point out that fasting is abstinence from anything that hinders communion with God. Then discuss the different forms of fasting mentioned in Scripture:

   a. Luke 4:2—abstaining from all food, as illustrated by Christ's fast following His baptism.

   b. Ezra 10:6—the absolute fast, abstaining from drinking as well as eating, illustrated by Ezra's fast as he mourned over the faithlessness of God's people in exile.

   c. 1 Corinthians 7:3–6—mutual consent of marriage partners to abstain from sexual relations for a specific time so they can devote themselves to prayer.

   What does Christ tell us should be our motive for fasting? Read Matthew 6:16–18. *Why should we do this?*

   Our motives for fasting must be right if we expect to see results. Discuss some wrong reasons for fasting. Remind the group that our fasting will be useless if it's done with the wrong motives.

2. Explain: "Throughout the Bible, God impressed on the hearts of His people the importance of fasting and praying. And every time people fasted and prayed, God released His supernatural power to bring about whatever was necessary to meet their

needs. Whether it was wisdom or the defeat of an enemy, God was always faithful to provide. Since God so mightily honored the prayers of those who fasted, we should make fasting a part of our lives as well."

Discuss the four principles of fasting:

a. Fasting may be used by God to expose sin, but we cannot use it to cover up sin. *Why is it futile for us to fast and pray, expecting God to answer, when we're harboring unconfessed sin of some kind?*

b. Fasting brings our physical appetites under the Holy Spirit's control. *Since our physical drives are God-given, why must we bring them under the Spirit's control when we're fasting? Can God-given drives, fulfilled within the boundaries of God's Word, ever be evil? If our drives get out of balance and we become their slaves, how can fasting help us get in balance again?*

c. Fasting brings our minds, wills, and emotions under the Spirit's control. *How can fasting aid us when we face big decisions?*

d. Fasting aids us when we seek God in worship. *How would fasting and seeking God in prayer on Saturday help us to worship Him in church on Sunday?*

3. In Matthew 6, Jesus did not say, "*If* you fast." He said, "*When*
   you fast." Why did Jesus fast? Read Mark 1:9–15.

   Jesus spoke of the closeness of His relationship with His
   Father (Matt. 11:27). Yet He still felt the need for separation
   from other people and life's ordinary pursuits to fast and pray.
   What message can we find in His example for ourselves?

   Why did Daniel fast? (Read Dan. 9:1–3.) *If we want God to
   answer the prayer of Psalm 25:4–5 for us, what changes might we
   have to make in our lives?*

   Why does God want us to fast at times as well as repent of sin?
   Find the pattern of confession and fasting in Ezra 9, Nehemiah
   9, and Daniel 9.

   *What were Nehemiah's priorities? What feelings prompted him
   to act?* Read Nehemiah 1:1–4; 2.

4. Hand out the 3" x 5" cards and pencils. Have each group member draw a line down the middle of the index card and write the
   following over column one: *Activity.* Over column two have each
   group member write: *Hours Spent.* Then ask members to jot down
   a list of their daily activities in the *Activity* column, including working, eating, sleeping, relaxing, exercising, socializing, etc. Finally,
   ask the group to fill in the *Hours Spent* daily on each activity.

   *How much time do you usually spend eating, working, study-
   ing, socializing, or sleeping? How much time do you spend with
   God—reading the Word, praying, and meditating? What relationship do you see between your spiritual strength and the time you
   spend with the Lord?*

5. *Do you have a need you believe God wants you to fast and pray about?* It may be a personal need—deliverance from a besetting sin or a desire to know God better—or a need you feel burdened about for your church or nation—or perhaps a need God wants you to pray about in someone else's life. *Are you willing to seek the Lord with prayer and fasting until He answers?* You may feel led to fast one meal a week, one day a week, or God may lead you to a two- or three-day fast, or even longer. *Are you willing to obey whatever He asks you to do?*

6. Ask members to spend time in silent prayers of commitment. Close with a prayer of faith that the Lord will enable each member to keep his or her commitment.

Activities Before Next Session

1. Read chapter 4.

2. Note any changes you want to make in your priorities this week as you schedule time for waiting on God in prayer. You must make time by deciding your priorities. Be aware of Satan's attacks and refuse to be conquered by them. Remember: "Greater is [God] that is in you, than [the Devil] that is in the world" (1 John 4:4).

SESSION 4
A PRAYER BURDEN
CHAPTER 4

Session Goals

1. To explore the scriptural meaning of praying with a burden.

2. To be aware of and on guard against Satan's tactics to sidetrack us from assuming and seeing through our prayer burden.

3. To sincerely promise God we are available to bear prayer burdens for Him.

Preparation

1. Have on hand paper and pencils for everyone.

2. Prepare opening and closing prayers related specifically to the material in this session.

Discussion

1. Hand out paper and pencils. Quickly sketch a "prayer wheel" on the chalkboard, whiteboard, or pad of paper. Draw a smaller circle in the middle of the prayer wheel, and spokes from the smaller inner circle to the outer wheel. Each spoke represents a prayer burden, so you might label each spoke *Home, Church, Friends, Work,* or *Nation.*

    Ask the members to draw their own prayer wheels. On the spokes, they should write requests they make often with little feeling or expectancy that God will answer. Perhaps they pray out of duty, but they put little of themselves into the requests.

    Say: "Scripture speaks of a different kind of prayer—a costly kind that is described as a burden. The word *burden* brings a picture to our minds of a heavy load that is hard to carry. We rarely hear of prayer burdens today, so we often pray burdenless prayers—repeating the same requests over and over with no sense of urgency."

2. Divide members into smaller groups (unless you're part of a small-enough group already). Have each small group explore the prayer burden described in Nehemiah 1—2 using the following questions:

    How would you describe a prayer burden that is from God? How did it affect Nehemiah? Toward what specific need was Nehemiah's burden directed? Why was his burden so intense? What kind of response did Nehemiah expect from God?

3. Reassemble in a large group and discuss five key principles you learned from reading chapter 4 of *Handle with Prayer* that relate to prayer burdens. Have each member describe a prayer burden. Be sure to point out that a burden is an inner sense of weight, which is an expression of God's concern regarding a particular need in a person's life.

   How can you tell the difference between simply being worried and having a prayer burden? Worry is self-centered and focuses on circumstances; a prayer burden is God-centered and focuses on God and what He can do.

   What two important principles can we draw from Nehemiah's experience of bearing a burden for God? First, a burden from God is always directed toward a specific need. Second, when God burdens our hearts to pray, it is evidence that He intends to do something about the matter.

   Why does God always look for a godly person He can trust to follow through with a prayer burden? God wants us involved with one another in a spiritual way. He wants us loving and encouraging one another. God allows us to be part of somebody else's blessing by allowing us to be part of the solution.

   How does Satan attack the person who receives a prayer burden to try to get him to forget about it?

4. *What determines the intensity of a burden?* Two things—the magnitude of the situation God wants to deal with and the immediacy with which God wants to deal with it.

   Should our prayer burdens be secrets between us and God, or should we discuss them with others? Some need to be shared, while others must be kept private. We must be sensitive to God's guidance when it comes to sharing burdens.

   What personal blessings come to us when we faithfully shoulder burdens? God's cleansing process in our lives results in a new sense of closeness to Him; we love Him more, serve Him more faithfully, and experience an increased love for others.

5. Review with the group Dr. Stanley's insights in the last four paragraphs of chapter 4. *Are you willing to be part of someone else's blessing by allowing God to make you part of the solution?* Pray the prayer in the second-to-last paragraph of chapter 4.

   Ask the group to silently consider: *Is there a need that God keeps bringing to your attention over and over? Have you tried to dismiss it or bury it or commit it briefly to the Lord?* Perhaps this is a burden God is asking you to bear for Him. Spend time now silently praying for that need.

6. Close with a time of silent prayer.

Activities Before Next Session

1. Read chapter 5.

2. Pray for your burden in time segments this week as the Lord impresses the need on your heart. Look expectantly for the answer.

3. Ask two members who will see each other before the next session to stage a conversation in a public place (over coffee at work; in a restaurant; among mutual friends; etc.) concerning Christian lifestyle. One should take the stance: "Christians are to live in poverty, suffer persecution, and die in poverty as a sacrifice for God." The other person should argue: "All we have to do is ask God, and He will pour out His blessings on us. He will give us whatever we ask for." These two members should be sensitive to the reactions of their listeners. The group members should be ready to report on their experiment at the next meeting.

SESSION 5
ANSWERED PRAYER
CHAPTER 5

Session Goals

1. To expose current prayer hang-ups concerning God's willingness to answer prayer.

2. To find and believe the scriptural grounds on which God will answer our prayers.

3. To move out of the up-and-down experiences of God's answers and His silence into the joyful one of answered prayer.

Preparation

1. Check with the two members you asked to stage the
   Christian-lifestyle conversation. They should be ready to
   tell the group what happened during this meeting.

2. Today, as always, you will need to allow time for prayer at
   the end of the session.

Discussion

1. Begin with a sharing time, emphasizing what God has done for
   His glory in individuals' prayer lives.

2. Brainstorm with the group some common prayer hang-ups. Jot
   down members' responses on the chalkboard, whiteboard, or
   pad of paper. Hang-ups will likely include: We shouldn't bother
   God about material things; we aren't worthy for God to answer;
   we shouldn't ask God for "little things" we can do for ourselves;
   when we sin, that's it—no more blessings from God.

   Make no comments about the responses at this point. They
   will be answered later in the session.

3. Ask the group to turn to Matthew 7:7–11 and read aloud
   Jesus' own encouragement to pray. Point out that in this passage, Jesus teaches us to build our relationships with Him
   through prayer, learning to trust Him and believing He wants
   to bless us.

Say: "In every area of life, the way to find what we are looking for is by talking to our heavenly Father." *How would you answer the Christian who says, "It's unspiritual to ask God for material things"?*

Explain that wise parents do everything in their power to satisfy the needs—material, nutritional, and spiritual—of their children. *Does God do less for His children?* We make the servant greater than the master when we decide how God will and will not bless us.

Discuss with the group how we are to build our relationships with God. Refer to Matthew 7:7.

How would you answer the person who says, "I don't deserve God's answers to my prayers"? Remind the group that God answers prayer on the basis of His love for us—not on our worthiness or deserving. We have already received His greatest Gift when we received His Son as our Savior. Certainly we can believe Him for life's minor things.

4. Ask the participants who staged a conversation in a public place to share the story of what happened. *What is the balance between these two false, extreme attitudes?* Read Psalm 37:4, and give Dr. Stanley's information under the first two paragraphs of "God's Attitude toward Blessing His Children" in chapter 5.

5. Read Psalm 66:18. *What does it mean to "regard iniquity" in our hearts?* Bring out Dr. Stanley's insight under the heading "Right Relationship" in chapter 5.

How do we use the key of faith as Jesus explained it in Mark 11:24? Jesus promised that whatever we are able to visualize by faith as ours, God will make it so.

6. Read John 14:14. *What does it mean to really pray in Jesus' name?* To pray in Jesus' name means to ask something because it is in character with what Jesus would ask if He were in our circumstances. *Why can we never ask for something in Jesus' name unless we are also fulfilling His requirement stated in John 15:7?* The request must be in keeping with His nature and character as He lives His life through us. Since He indwells us, He not only desires to live through us but to intercede through us as well.

   What attitude must we hold when naming requests (James 1:5–6)? How do we get it? Note Dr. Stanley's explanation in the first two paragraphs of "Right Attitudes" in chapter 5.

   What is the right motive to have when we ask for something (Matt. 5:16)?

7. Now ask for specific prayer requests concerning personal needs, national needs, church needs, etc. Then pair off members. Spend several minutes allowing group members to pray for one another according to the insights given in chapter 5. Challenge the group to look expectantly for God's answers this week and in the future.

Activities Before Next Session

1. Read chapter 6.

2. Encourage group members to check on other group members who are in need during the week.

SESSION 6
WHY OUR PRAYERS ARE UNANSWERED
CHAPTER 6

Session Goals

1. To explore scriptural reasons why God does not answer prayers.

2. To note areas of our lives that we must deal with before God will answer, or sometimes even hear, our prayers.

3. To check out our unanswered prayers with the Lord and ask Him why He is not responding.

4. To commit ourselves to making unhindered, two-way communication with God our first priority.

Preparation

1. Study chapter 6 and apply it to yourself.

2. Continue the theme of problems concerning answers to prayer by typing or writing out the following six problems and their corresponding Scriptures (the complete verses, not just the references) on twelve individual slips of paper.

Fold the slips and put them into a small box so the first twelve members to arrive can draw one slip each (six problems, six Scripture verses) as they enter the room. If your group doesn't have twelve members, let participants draw from the six problems first. Then let them draw from the scriptural answers, so that each member has at least one slip of paper. You should be prepared to read the answers for any leftover slips. Tell members to wait until the appropriate time to reveal what is on their papers.

> *Problem 1:* I got mad this week so I quit praying. God won't hear me anymore.
> *Answer 1:* Psalm 66:18; 1 John 1:9

> *Problem 2:* I don't know if God blessed the people I prayed for or not.
> *Answer 2:* Mark 11:24

> *Problem 3:* I'm afraid God won't give me what I asked for.
> *Answer 3:* 1 John 5:14

Problem 4: I prayed in Jesus' name, but God didn't answer.
Answer 4: John 14:14; 15:7

Problem 5: My friend told me I shouldn't ask God for the
thing I was praying for. Now I don't know what to do.
Answer 5: James 1:5–6

Problem 6: I'm embarrassed to tell anyone what I asked
God for. It was such a little request.
Answer 6: Matthew 5:16

3. Have on hand pencils and paper, or chalkboard/whiteboard
   and chalk/markers, for group use in discussion point 3.

4. Time the segments of your session carefully so that the
   group will have time to spend in prayer at the end of the
   meeting.

Discussion

1. Say: "Have you ever wished you could go to a spiritual clinic
   when your prayers were ailing? Let's pretend we can do that
   today. Several 'patients' will tell us their prayer problems and
   we'll hear from the Word how they can get help."

   Ask the six persons to read their prayer problems from their
   slips of paper. Have the group members read aloud the six
   Scripture references that correspond to each verse. You should

be ready to read any verses that were not distributed to members of the group.

2. Tell Frances's story (or a similar one you know of personally) from the opening portion of chapter 6. Say: "We can't ignore hurts like these. We don't want glib answers. Instead, we turn to the Lord who promised that we are not slaves, but friends."

   Read John 15:15, or have someone from the group read it aloud.

   Also, read this passage from chapter 6 of *Handle with Prayer*: "Prayer is a child making a request of the Father. And just like any good earthly father, our heavenly Father is willing to tell us why we cannot have certain things. But before He will tell us, we must ask (James 4:2)."

3. Let's look at several reasons why our prayers are not answered. Naturally if we have unconfessed sin in our lives, our prayers will not be answered. *But what other reasons keep our prayers from being answered?*

   Divide your group members into two smaller groups. Appoint a leader for each and give them these assignments:

   Group 1: Study the first half of chapter 6, the sections titled "We Must Seek God"; "We Must Trust Him"; "He Is Preparing Us"; and "Sometimes God Has Something Better." Be ready to present (via skits, drawings, chalkboard sketches, etc.) four reasons why prayers are not answered.

Group 2: Study the second half of chapter 6, the sections titled "Family Relationships"; "We Must Check Our Motives"; "We Must Have Unwavering Faith"; "Focus on His Word"; "Selfishness Hinders Our Prayers"; "Indifference to God's Word"; and "Unconfessed Sin." Be ready to present (via skits, drawings, chalkboard or whiteboard sketches, etc.) seven reasons why prayers are not answered.

Allow the groups ten to twelve minutes to prepare.

Then ask members from group 1 to present their report. Their four reasons should come directly from the titles of the four sections of the text that they reviewed. They may want to include other key concepts from these sections in their presentation as well.

Remind members that we should keep in mind the big picture of God's will when we pray. Ask the group to silently consider if the goal of their lives is God Himself—knowing and loving Him—*or receiving His gifts.*

Members from group 2 should present their report next.

Their seven reasons should come from the titles of the seven sections of the text that they reviewed. As with group 1, this group may also want to include other key ideas from the text in their presentation.

4. Summarize or read the last paragraph of chapter 6 to the group. Then spend a few minutes in silent prayer as a group, allowing time for the Lord to deal with members individually.

If time allows, conclude with prayers of thanksgiving and praise. Ask members to use audible prayers to thank the Lord for the insights He has given, the cleansing He has done, and the promises He has extended.

Activities Before Next Session

1. Read chapter 7.

2. Encourage group members to seek out Scripture during the coming week. If they encounter a problem during the week and find a particular Scripture reference that helps them, ask them to share their stories with you or other members of the group.

SESSION 7
HOW TO PRAY IN THE WILL OF GOD
CHAPTER 7

Session Goals

1. To investigate the scriptural basis for knowing how to pray according to God's will.

2. To recognize and learn how to reject Satan's attempts to thwart our prayers.

3. To make requests in God's will and receive His answers.

Preparation

1. Study chapter 7 of the text. How have the truths explored there helped you personally know how to pray in God's will and receive answers? What personal victories and

failures (from which you learned better how to pray) can
you share with your group?

2. Assemble chalkboard and chalk or whiteboard and markers.

Discussion

1. Ask for personal testimonies of times when members prayed
with confidence that what they were asking was in God's will.
They should also share how God answered their prayers.

   *How did these experiences differ from those times when you
   prayed, without any assurance that you were praying in God's will?
   What made the difference?*

   It is discouraging to persist in prayer when we aren't sure
   our requests are compatible with God's plan. But our whole
   attitude changes to joyful expectancy when we go to the Father
   with unwavering confidence that our requests have His divine
   approval. And this is how He wants us to pray. In His Word He
   gives us clear instructions for praying in His will.

2. Read Matthew 7:7–11 and Philippians 4:6. *How do we know
   God wants us to ask Him for whatever we need? What one condition
   does God put on our prayers for our own good?* Refer to 1 John 5:14.

   Some requests are always in God's will, for He has told us
   so. *What are they?* Read Luke 19:10; Ephesians 4:32; 1 John
   3:17–18. Salvation of sinners; forgiving attitude toward those
   who wrong us; helping those who need food, shelter, clothing.

Sometimes we may not be certain that our prayer requests agree with God's will. But He has given us guidelines to find His will in prayer. *What threefold promise has God made concerning His response to our requests (1 John 5:14–15)?*

a. God listens when we pray according to His will.

b. We already possess what we have asked for.

c. We *know* that we have the petitions we desire of Him.

What three roadblocks does Satan throw in the way of the believer who is determined to pray according to God's will? What three principles will defeat Satan's roadblocks?

Satan's Stumbling Blocks	**Prayer Principles**
a. How can you make a request in faith when you don't know if God is in agreement with you?	We have the right to ask God what His will is (James 1:5).
b. Why waste your time praying if you aren't sure that God agrees with you?	The Holy Spirit prays through us when we don't understand what to pray, and at the same time, gives us understanding if we open up ourselves to Him (Rom. 8:26).
c. Look at your past. You don't have the right to ask God for anything; He won't listen to you.	God hears us because of Jesus' righteousness in us. Rather than focusing on ourselves, we are to persist in prayer, and God will reveal His will to us (John 16:13).

3. The following discussion lends itself well to an illustrated chalkboard, whiteboard, or easel pad discussion. Write the following
points for everyone to see.

Point 1: We must distinguish exactly what we are asking
God for—is it a want, a need, a request for direction?

Point 2: We should ask God to give us a passage of
Scripture that relates in some way to our request—a passage
we can meditate on, pray by, and live by until God grants our
request.

Point 3: We know that God wants to show us His will in
prayer and that if we are praying in His will, our prayers are
already answered. Therefore we should begin thanking Him.

Point 4: We must wait, not asking persistently for the same
thing, but using the Word God gave us as an anchor.

Point 5: We can enjoy God's peace (Phil. 4:6–7) because we
know we have prayed according to His will.

Sum up the lesson concepts presented in this passage at the
end of chapter 7: "God desires to give us direction in our prayers.
He has promised in His Word to do so. Our responsibility is to
seek His direction through Scripture. Once we have found His
promise to us, we must dig in and wait while thanking Him for

what is already ours. For 'if God be for us' (Rom. 8:31) in our prayers, who or what can stand against us?"

Challenge the group to consider the request that comes to their minds every time they pray. Members should ask the Lord silently and individually: *Lord, what is Your will concerning this request? What Scripture will You give me as an anchor?*

4. Have a time of silent prayer while members apply this session's concepts to their requests.

Close with audible prayer of thanksgiving that we can "be filled with the knowledge of [God's] will in all wisdom and spiritual understanding" (Col. 1:9).

Activities Before Next Session

1. Read chapter 8.

2. Encourage members to follow through with praying according to God's will in their specific requests until they have God's literal answers.

SESSION 8
A TIME TO WAIT, A TIME TO ACT
CHAPTER 8

Session Goals

1. To be able to discern when God says, "Wait," and when He says, "Move ahead."

2. To study scriptural principles concerning God's directions so that we can move back into the way of victory, especially if we have wallowed in defeat.

3. To deal with the point of divine conflict that will cheat us out of the success God desires for us in our prayer lives.

Preparation

1. Reread chapter 8 of the text. Look at goal 3 again. Is there some point of divine conflict that you have been afraid of or unwilling to deal with in your life? Can you see now why God has not answered your most persistent prayer—the one that occupies most of your prayer time? Is your rejection of God's expressed desire worth the emotional and spiritual (perhaps even physical) suffering you are enduring?

2. Have on hand chalkboard and chalk or whiteboard and markers, eraser, poster board (see discussion point 1), fiber-tip pens, paper, and pencils.

3. Make a copy of the Bible study instructions under discussion point 2 for each group leader or "battle commander."

Discussion

1. Write the title *Three Prayer Clocks* on the chalkboard or on a large sheet of poster board. Underneath the title, write the subpoints: *Stop, Wait,* and *Move Ahead.* Mention that there are times in all of our lives when God wants us to wait, as we discussed in session 7. But there are also times when God says, "Get up and do something. This is no time to be praying."

2. Divide members into two groups. Appoint a "battle commander" for each, and give each group commander the following instructions for his or her group, along with paper and pencils. (You already made copies. See preparation point 3.)

Group 1: Study Joshua 6 and draw up the battle strategy for taking the city of Jericho. *Why did the strategy work? What principles is God revealing to His children who face spiritual enemies?*

Group 2: Study Joshua 7 and draw up the battle strategy for taking the city of Ai. *Why did the strategy fail? What principles is God revealing to His children who face spiritual enemies?*

Allow ten to twelve minutes for smaller group discussion.

Then reassemble members and ask them to contrast the strategy and principles from the two battles. Note their comments on the chalkboard/whiteboard.

Jericho	Ai

Jericho

Strategy

Dictated by God to Commander Joshua: March around city once for six days; on the seventh day march around it seven times blowing a trumpet.

Result

Overwhelming victory.

Principles

a. There's a time to act and a time to wait.

b. We can't blame God for our problems.

c. The area we need to correct in our lives will probably not relate to what we're praying about.

d. Late obedience is disobedience.

e. Blessing follows obedience.

Ai

Strategy

Dictated by Commander Joshua after taking advice of his cohorts: Send spies into the city; spies returned confident that victory would be a pushover.

Result

Appalling defeat.

Principles

a. When we move ahead without consulting God, we experience defeat.

b. By taking the credit for our victories, we leave ourselves open for defeat.

c. We should not dwell on our past victories and become proud and overconfident.

d. We will be defeated when we fall into Satan's trap of pride.

e. Failure results from sin.

3. Ask the group to turn to Joshua 7:7–15. Let two people read aloud the dialogue between God and Joshua.

Based on last session's insights about how to pray in the will of God, what was lacking in Joshua's prayer? Point out that Joshua did not mention a promise from God he was relying on; he didn't thank God for the good things He had already done; he didn't praise God. Instead, he cried out in defeat and blamed God for getting him into the mess.

What did God say to Joshua? What mistakes do we make when things don't go as we think they should in our prayer lives? We talk too much and don't listen enough to God; we develop an attitude like Joshua's that blames God for our predicament.

What principle can we count on when things go wrong? The "Ai's" in our lives are not lost because of some slipup on God's part, but because of wrong things in our own lives.

What is the remedy? We should ask God to show us the source of our failure—correcting an unloving relationship, paying a debt, etc. *What is God's real concern?* He is concerned about our obedience to the initial prompting of His Spirit. *What light does James 4:17 throw on our predicament?*

4. Can you recall an incident when you prayed because you couldn't bring yourself to act? If members seem hesitant to share their experiences, tell them about a time you prayed when you should have taken action. Why is praying useless when God says, "Move"?

5. Spend time in silent prayer while each member assesses his or her own "Ai" and determines what to do about it. Close with an affirmation of victory, which always follows obedience.

Activities Before Next Session

1. State: "Perhaps most of us have determined that we will deal with our source of defeat as soon as possible. Satan will do all in his power to keep you from following through with your determination. He will say, 'Don't be a fool. What will people think if you do that?' (Such as: paying an old debt; apologizing for a wrong attitude, action, word; etc.) 'Cool it. Pray some more before you act; be sure it's God's voice you obey.' Ignore Satan, be true to your commitment, and enjoy God's victory blessing."

2. Read chapter 9.

3. Assign these four reports to members for presentation at the next meeting:

   a. *Public officials and national need.* This report should focus on the effect public officials have on the nation's morals. Ask the reporter(s) to bring examples from current news stories, which will give a fairly accurate picture of the moral climate of the nation.

   b. *The suffering church.* Research the church around the world and bring stories of suffering and persecution. Voice of the Martyrs is a good source of information concerning the life of the church in difficult parts of the world.

c. *Vocational servants.* This should be a sensitive report on missionaries, pastors, and other Christian workers and their emotional, spiritual, physical, or material needs. What are their goals? Their struggles? Their hurts? Their triumphs?

d. *Unsaved persons.* Ask a member (or someone else within your church) to give concrete examples of being burdened for an unsaved person and seeing that burden through. What part did prayer play in the experience?

SESSION 9
PRAYING FOR OTHERS
CHAPTER 9

Session Goals

1. To keep in mind those people for whom Scripture instructs us to pray.

2. To be aware of our privilege and responsibility of praying for others.

3. To spend time in intercessory prayer.

Preparation

1. Note that we will take two sessions—sessions 9 and 10—to unpack chapter 9 of *Handle with Prayer* and develop the important concept of intercession.

2. Have on hand paper, pencils, chalkboard and chalk, or whiteboard and markers.

3. Check with the four people who have been assigned special reports (see activity 3 in session 8). Make sure they are ready to share their findings at this meeting.

Discussion

1. Say: "It has often been said that we can give without loving, but we cannot love without giving. To give is a part of love, as the Lord of love has demonstrated to us over and over. Isn't the same true of prayer? We can pray without loving from a sense of duty or from a desire to be praised of men. But we can't love with Christ's sacrificial love without praying for the loved one(s). Our deepest desires for the loved one(s) should center in their relationship to God and His gifts. Praying for them is a part of loving them."

   Do you agree?

2. Distribute paper and pencils to members. Then call for the report on public officials and national need. As the group member gives his or her report, the group may jot down relational ideas the report generates.

   Read 1 Timothy 2:2. *Whom should we include in our prayers for those in authority?* We should include the president, congress, mayor, and our bosses. *How would giving thanks for a boss we think is unfair change our attitude toward him? How would this make it easier for us to work under him? How would you answer believers who think that public officials are all corrupt and prayer won't change anything (vv. 3–4)?*

Comment: "The moral decline in America, corruption in high places, loss of credibility among our leaders, and loss of faith in them require renewed commitment on our part to pray for our leaders" (chapter 9 of *Handle with Prayer*).

3. Ask for the report on the suffering church.

After the group member gives his or her report, point out that we are to pray for Christians who are persecuted, financially poor, spiritually lukewarm, and spiritually cold. (See "The Body of Christ" section in chapter 9.) *How can we make Philippians 1:27 a reality in our lives?*

4. Have the member who researched vocational servants in the church present his or her report. Read Ephesians 6:19. *What three requests are we to make for vocational servants?* That God would show His servants what to preach and teach; that they would speak the truth unashamedly and uncompromisingly; and that they would have the ability to make their messages clear.

What practical changes would take place if believers interceded for, rather than criticized, their pastors?

5. *How can our prayers change the destinies of God-called workers who are struggling with the discipline of obedience? If you are a*

worker, can you name the person(s) who prayed you out into your work?

6. Ask for the report on unsaved persons. *How will believing in 1 Timothy 2:4–6 change your prayers for the lost? Do you have specific names on your prayer list now? If not, why not?*

7. *How will practicing the principle of Matthew 5:44 make you a happier person? What will it do for your enemies?*

8. Silently evaluate the time you spend praying for your family and close friends. To help yourself and the group members with the evaluation, consider these questions: *How much time do you spend praying for people outside your inner circle? Authority figures? The church around the world? Do you pray for any people in prison for their faith? Any unsaved people? What do your prayers reveal about your unselfishness or selfishness?*

9. Divide members into small groups. Exchange requests concerning the persons discussed in this session. Pray for definite requests in the small groups.

Activities Before Next Session

1. Continue with your intercessory prayer requests.

2. Reread chapter 9.

SESSION 10
PRAYING FOR OTHERS
CHAPTER 9

Session Goals

1. To learn how to pray effectively and expectantly for others.

2. To follow up insights with definite requests and prayers.

Preparation

1. Reread chapter 9 and be ready to share your most effective resource tool in prayer (see discussion point 1).

2. Have on hand chalkboard and chalk or whiteboard and markers, paper and pencils.

3. Analyze the three prayers found in Ephesians 1:16–23;

3:14–21; and Colossians 1:9–14 according to the instructions in discussion point 3.

Discussion

1. Ask members to tell what methods of praying expectantly they have found the most effective.

    Some may keep prayer journals; others may keep prayer lists; still others may make diary notations. Challenge the group to decide what resource they think would be most effective for them to keep track of prayers, and encourage them to begin using that resource consistently if they are not already doing so.

2. Draw from Dr. Stanley's insights in chapter 9, your personal experiences, and other biblical insights on prayer to answer the following questions as a group. *What does it mean to pray with "a heart of compassion"?*

    Why must we be able to identify with a person's need before we can pray effectively for that person? What can we learn from Christ's unreserved identification with us (Heb. 4:15)?

    What is one of the primary reasons God allows His children to suffer (2 Cor. 1:4)? How has suffering helped you in your intercession for others?

    What are some ways we can become part of the answer we are asking God for in intercessory prayer? (Note the "Being Part of the Answer" section in chapter 9.) *Can you relate specific experiences when this has been true of you?*

3. Divide members into three groups. Hand out paper and pencils and ask each group to analyze its assigned prayer to find specific requests, needs the prayer brings out, and feelings expressed in the prayer about God and the Son.

Group 1: Study Ephesians 1:16–23.

Group 2: Study Ephesians 3:14–21.

Group 3: Study Colossians 1:9–14.

Allow ten to twelve minutes for the groups to study their prayers. Then call for their findings. As the groups respond, compare and contrast the three prayers on the chalkboard/ whiteboard using these captions: *Specific Requests; Probable Needs; Praise and Thanksgiving.*

Mention that Paul prayed these prayers for believers who, like us, lived in a hostile world, loved, suffered, won victories, and experienced defeats. *From these three prayers, what should we incorporate into our intercessory prayers?*

Read: "We lie when we flippantly say to people, 'I love you,' and then forget to pray for them in their times of need. Yet how many times has someone asked us to pray about a specific need and we say, 'I'll be praying for you'—then we pray for him or her casually, if we remember the prayer request at all? We need to examine ourselves and see if we really know what love is all about. We will pray consistently for those we really love. This is the reason our prayers are so often full of our own desires and needs" (chapter 9 of *Handle with Prayer*).

4. Pair off members.

Each pair should mention specific prayer burdens for others. Then they should pray sentence prayers for each need. Praying sentence prayers means that no one monopolizes the prayer time, but individuals pray specifically and briefly about a request while their partners pick up where they left off. An amazing number of requests can be covered in this manner, and the prayer time remains fresh and stimulating and each member has equal time with God.

Challenge group members to tell God they are willing to be part of the answer to the requests they are praying for. They should ask Him for a spirit of love and compassion for those in need.

5. Close with an audible prayer of thanksgiving for answers all will see when God responds according to His Word.

Activities Before Next Session

1. During the week, continue to pray through requests mentioned today by your partner.

2. Read chapter 10.

SESSION 11
PRAYER IS WHERE THE ACTION IS
CHAPTER 10

Session Goals

1. To look at a scriptural example of prayer partners and what they accomplished.

2. To know that life's real battles are won and lost in the place of prayer, not on life's battlefield.

3. To determine to develop prayer partners and be the kind of person others will want for theirs.

Preparation

1. Reread chapter 10 of the text. Have you had persons who prayed especially for you while you've been leading these

sessions? If so, how have you felt the effectiveness of their prayers? Are you someone's prayer partner? What have you shared in the way of joy, sorrow, and victories as you met for prayer?

2. Assemble chalkboard and chalk, or whiteboard and markers.

Discussion

1. Open the session with the following statements:

- Quiet, passive people find it easier to pray than active, aggressive people.

- Life's battles are won and lost in the place of prayer, not on the battlefield of everyday life.

Ask members for their reactions to these statements. Help your group note that temperament is never an excuse for knowing or not knowing God. Scripture gives us a good picture of David (who was both a poet and a warrior) and Paul (who was an aggressive activist by nature). Both men loved the Lord deeply and gave us the most graphic descriptions of their devotion in their writings. Psalms 23 and 63 reveal some of David's longings for God. Paul's life philosophy is given in Philippians 3:7–14, where he unashamedly admits that Christ is everything to him.

2. Ask the group to turn to Exodus 17:8–13. *What is the background of the incident in this passage?* Refer to the opening paragraph of chapter 10 in *Handle with Prayer.*

   What were Moses' instructions to Joshua (v. 9)? Why did God give the Israelites victory?

   What three principles can you draw from this incident that will make your prayer life more exciting and fruitful? Life's battles are won and lost in the place of prayer, not on the battlefields of everyday life; we can become weary in life's battles—too tired to pray effectively; we need an Aaron and a Hur as prayer partners to share our burdens and pray for our needs.

3. *How does the principle of "Life's battles are won through prayer" help us evaluate the success or failure of a church? Where does God win His battles in churches?* See Dr. Stanley's insights in the second paragraph under "Where the Battle Is Won" in chapter 10.

   What lesson can we learn from Old Testament saints who were placed in arenas where they faced overwhelming disadvantages? Explain that in a spirit of total dependence upon God and unwavering faith in Him, they fought the real battles on their faces in prayer. Their public victory was the outcome of private victory.

   What message does this have for us today? Refer to the last three paragraphs of the section "Where the Battle Is Won."

   How can church conflicts get resolved? Through faith in God and relying on Him to fight our battles, we claim our victory in private on our knees before the public battles ever begin.

Why do we faint and grow weary? Explain that sometimes we see our problems as so big that they block our view of God. *How does God view our human weaknesses? What is God's solution to our problem of fainting and growing weary when we should be strong and praying?* God built His church on a system of interdependence—each person ministering to others through different talents, gifts, abilities, and prayers. At the same time, all recognize God as the source of blessings. God is the source of power; people are instruments He uses.

What do we learn about the need of prayer support from others when Christ is praying in the garden of Gethsemane?

4. Read Ecclesiastes 4:10. Discuss the concept expressed under "A Threefold Cord" in chapter 10 of *Handle with Prayer.* Then jot down qualifications of prayer partners on the board as you discuss them: spiritually minded; warriors—not counselors; compassionate; and faithful.

    Ask the group if they have prayer partners. If so, ask them to share a few of their defeats, victories, and insights.

    Say: "You need one or two others to bear your burdens with you. Are you willing to ask the Lord to send you a prayer partner? Are you willing to be a prayer partner to someone else?"

5. Spend time in prayer as the Spirit leads you and as you sense the needs of your group members.

Activities Before Next Session

1. You might want to delve deeper into your spiritual response to becoming a prayer partner. Are you willing to pay the price of time and devotion to become one? If you aren't willing, can you justly ask God to lay your need on someone else's heart?

2. Read chapter 11 of the text.

SESSION 12
THE WARFARE OF PRAYER
CHAPTER 11

Session Goals

1. To realize the nature of the spiritual conflict every believer faces.

2. To put on the whole armor of God so that we will be spiritually prepared to engage in the conflict.

3. To acknowledge and tear down any strongholds of sin in our lives through Spirit-filled prayer.

Preparation

1. Reread chapter 11 of *Handle with Prayer* and personally apply the goals for this session.

2. Assemble chalkboard and chalk or whiteboard and markers.

Discussion

1. Give the concepts of the first three paragraphs in chapter 11. *What are the different aspects of prayer?* Asking, receiving, thanksgiving, praise, and warfare. *Who is our enemy?* Satan. *What is our equipment?* God's armor.

2. On the chalkboard or whiteboard, ask the group to contrast the tensions the Christians faced while living in the Roman Empire with those we face today. *How are they similar or different?*

3. *What is the ministry of the church? Why has the church recoiled from such warfare? What do many churches think is their only responsibility?* Leading people to Christ.

   What other responsibilities does the church have? How has God equipped His church for the task Christ gave her in Matthew 28:19–20? Bring out Dr. Stanley's insights under the section "Equipped for the Task" in chapter 11.

   Read Matthew 12:29; 16:19; 18:18. *How did Jesus sum up the essence of spiritual warfare?*

4. Read this passage from chapter 11 of *Handle with Prayer*: "Paul makes it clear that we are not coming against people or circumstances in this war, for Satan and his host are our enemy (Eph.

6:11–12). This is a spiritual conflict, and therefore, we must be spiritually prepared. We must have on the whole armor of God. And if we are going to put it on, we must understand what it is."

What does it mean to gird our loins with truth? What is the breastplate of righteousness, and how do we put it on?

How do we use the sword of the Spirit in our warfare? The Word of God is a weapon to be used to defeat Satan. We should use specific Scriptures to deal with specific attacks. Then as we saturate our prayers with these Scriptures, we can bind Satan from our lives.

5. The essence of spiritual warfare is binding and loosing (Matt. 16:19). *What are we to bind and loose (2 Cor. 10:4–5)? What is a stronghold?* (An area of sin that has become so ingrained in a person's life that it has become a part of his or her lifestyle.) Ask members to name some specific strongholds. (Such as habits—drugs, fornication, smoking, overeating; or attitudes—rejection, loneliness, worry, doubt.)

How can we tear down strongholds that are imprisoning the lost? We should ask God to reveal specific strongholds that are keeping the lost from accepting Christ. Then by God's authority, we can cast down those strongholds and ask God to send His Spirit of conviction into those parts of their lives.

6. Read the last two paragraphs of chapter 11 to the group. Ask members to examine their lives for strongholds that are

imprisoning them. Challenge them to tear down those strongholds now and to put on the whole armor of God.

7. Close this session by joining with group members and praying.

Activities Before Next Session

1. Instruct members to review chapter 11 and make note of
   any portions that they feel need more discussion.

2. Ask members to evaluate their own prayer lives. They
   should consider how they've grown and how their ideas
   about prayer have changed during these sessions.

SESSION 13
REVIEW

Session Goals

1. To review the entire text of *Handle with Prayer.*

2. To challenge members to apply the lessons they've learned to their own prayer lives.

Preparation

1. Review the session goals for each of the previous twelve sessions. Ask the Holy Spirit to give you insight as to which goals you should reinforce during this last session.

2. Carefully review the text of *Handle with Prayer.* Make note of any portions that you didn't discuss with your group and be ready to talk about them at this meeting. Also be

ready to discuss any sections that the group seemed to
have difficulty understanding or accepting.

3. Prepare a brief summary of the text (one or two sentences
   for each chapter). Be ready to present it in your review
   with the group.

4. Pray specifically for each group member. Ask God to make
   you sensitive to their individual needs and to use you to
   speak to them during this session.

Discussion

1. Open the session with the brief summary you prepared. Ask
   members what concepts they feel need more discussion.

2. Ask members to share what has been most helpful about these
   sessions. If members seem hesitant, tell them about what you've
   learned and applied to your own prayer life. Then ask them
   how they have grown in their understanding of the concept of
   prayer.
   *How have they grown in the closeness of their relationships with
   God? In their caring for one another? In their willingness to hear others' burdens? In their assuming their place in the warfare of prayer?*

3. Ask for prayer requests. Spend time praying for these requests
   with the group.

4. Challenge members to continue with their prayer notebooks, recording specific prayer requests and answers.